CHANGE
My thirty-five years in AFRICA

PETER J. BRASHLER

Tyndale House
Publishers, Inc.
Wheaton, Illinois

LIBRARY OF CONGRESS CATALOG CARD NUMBER 79-63196
ISBN 0-8423-0220-4, PAPER.
COPYRIGHT © 1979 BY PETER J. BRASHLER. ALL RIGHTS
RESERVED.
FIRST PRINTING, AUGUST 1979.
PRINTED IN THE UNITED STATES OF AMERICA.

CHANGE
My 35 Years in Africa

Peter & Edythe Brashler

Gal. 6:14

To the Africa Inland Mission

CONTENTS

FOREWORD

With the possible exception of politicians, probably no group of human beings have been more frequently or more thoroughly caricatured than missionaries. From the halo/pedestal mirage on the one hand, to the shorts/pith helmet/Bible/palm tree image on the other, missionaries are generally considered either saints or insensitive destroyers of primitive cultures.

Dr. Brashler is guilty of neither of these extremes in his portrayal of nearly forty years of missionary life and experiences in the Congo. The humanity of the missionary comes through loud and clear, with frank admissions of resistance to God's call, struggling with the smoking habit, apprehensions about raising support, discouragement from malaria, struggles with cultural adaptation and language learning, and the evaporation of a supposed love for the Africans.

Pete and Edythe Brashler went to Africa in 1940, and spent six eventful and fruitful terms, returning to the States for retirement in 1976. The chronicle is therefore politically and culturally significant in that it spans both colonial and independent Africa. Dr. Brashler's insights into developing situations complex with factors of nationalism, communism, racism, and religious conflict are very helpful to an understanding of Africa, and, in my view, very accurate.

Years of general missionary work, ten years of teaching in a school for training African pastors and evangelists, and fourteen years as Field Director of some 135 missionaries in Africa Inland Mission's Congo field (now Zaire) have given him a broad and deep understanding of the whole missions scene in that land. My close and personal association with the Brashlers for ten of those years in the Bible School at Adi contributed greatly to my nostalgia as I read, and to my appreciation of the first class journalistic job Pete has done in sharing his and Edythe's experiences with us. I gladly acknowledge Pete's wide understanding of African cultures, his unusual ability linguistically as he learned to speak fluently in French, Flemish, Bangala, Swahili, and Kakwa, and his obvious flair for stimulating and interesting verbal communication.

This volume could well be subtitled "A Light-Hearted Chronicle of Missionary Life." Pete's highly developed sense of humor pops out of every page. He has a unique ability to laugh at himself, and his portrayals of the missionary "saint" dropping through the privy hole, the African Christians poking fun at their bumbling missionary, and many humorous incidents which took place in bizarre Bunia and other places make this book a delight to read.

But it's not simply entertainment! The heart burden to reach those not knowing the love of God through Christ shines through, as does the joy of seeing the power of God at work transforming lives, the excitement of trusting God to work miracles in the midst of chaotic situations where man's best, or worst, resulted in sheer anarchy, and the shared joy of the day the full Bangala Bible arrived at Adi.

This volume will delight your heart, inform your mind, and challenge your will to become involved with God in world evangelization.

Peter Stam
U. S. Director
Africa Inland Mission
January 1979

ACKNOWLEDGMENTS

I wish to express my warm appreciation to Captain Ken Dodson and his wife Letha, for their advice and encouragement, and to Gertrude Carlson, Marge Benthine, and Verona Hanson, for their help in typing the manuscript.

Above all, I thank my wife, Edythe, for her loving support in this project.

ONE
THE ORDER
OF THE LEOPARD

The Zairian *commissaire de zone* stepped out of his Mercedes at the Blukwa mission station. A crowd of blacks pressed around his car. Obviously he had official business to transact.

I invited the dignitary into the house where all the missionaries were assembled. Only a short time before, Edythe and I had arrived from Bunia, our home and field office headquarters, to discuss mission personnel matters at the Blukwa station. The commissaire looked into the house and replied, *"Mais non, monsieur. Je voudrais vous voir tout seul."* He wanted to see the mission's field director in private to settle a very important matter.

I took him to another house where we could talk without interruption. He opened his exotic attaché case and selected a folder marked "PLAINTE-SUBVERSIVE - BRASHLER." Spreading open the dossier, he produced an ominous-looking document which he handed to me.

"Monsieur," he began, "I have a list of very serious accusations against you. You are accused of being a subversive, anti-Mobutu, antirevolutionary, opposed to the MPR (Mouvement Populaire de la Revolution—the one and only political party), opposed to the government policy of the restoration of authentic Zairian culture, resistant to the decree of abandoning the use of Christian names. And you are involved in an attempt at a coup d'etat. Here, take a look at these accusations."

Those were all trumped-up charges, but they fit into the pattern of eliminating "imperialists." After all, missionaries were a hangover of the old colonialist government in the Belgian Congo and had worked hand-in-glove with it throughout the years. The Belgians had long since been eliminated, but the missionaries were still around to exploit the citizens of Zaire (the country's new name). Now, every last vestige of colonialism must go. Independence must come to the church as well as to the government.

I noted that the charges were made because of a conference held at Blukwa some three months earlier. At that time the thriving church here had decided to have a five-day conference to study the prophecies of Christ's return. They had invited Edythe and me to speak on the subject each morning.

Such a conclave could not be held without first getting permission from the commissaire, and without having government observers from the political party on hand to take a full report to the commissaire's office. All of those requirements had been observed, however, and the conference was tremendously successful.

Crowds of people came on foot or by bicycle, a few by car or truck. There were women wearing bright-colored prints with political slogans painted on them, and men with Mobutu shirts. The MPR was represented by about six observers, on hand for every meeting, ready with their notebooks to record everything that took place. These officials were friendly, and they accepted the church's hospitality by eating voraciously and vociferously the meals provided for them.

During my messages I had spoken about the Lord's return and his setting up his kingdom. I emphasized that he was coming to punish sin and to establish a regime of righteousness and peace. All of this made sense to the believers, and many Zairians responded to the gospel invitation. There was no complaint from the official observers during the conference.

Now, three months later, the commissaire himself had come to Blukwa to lower the boom on the director of the 115 Africa Inland Mission missionaries working in Zaire. Com-

pletely astounded after reading over the half dozen complaints, I handed them back to him.

The commissaire continued. "These are very serious
charges, and are contemptible in the eyes of the government.
What do you have to say in your defense?"

Accusations of being anti-Mobutu, antigovernment, and
subversive were indeed very serious. They could be interpreted
as treason, and could easily land me in prison. Just then it
seemed that the Holy Spirit beeped a message into my mind. I
recalled the words of Jesus. "But beware of men: for they will
deliver you up . . . And ye shall be brought before governors
and kings for my sake. . . . But when they deliver you up, take
no thought how or what ye shall speak: for it shall be given you
in that same hour what ye shall speak" (Mt. 10:17-19).

"Are you guilty of these charges?" The commissaire re-
lentlessly resumed his assault.

"*Monsieur le commissaire,*" came my response, "I want
you to know that I have served as a missionary in your country since 1940. Never once have I been arrested on any charge.
Nor have I been anything but cooperative with every government decree. I invite you to come with me to Bunia to the
commissaire sous-regional, who is your superior, and who
has known me for years. He will tell you all about me.

"As to these charges," I continued, "the messages in question are all on tape, and I invite you to listen to them yourself. I challenge you to call the pastor of the church and the
elders, who can give you a firsthand account of all that took
place at the conference. Regarding the six accusations, I cate-
gorically deny each one of them."

"*Eh bien!*" fumed the commissaire, "Now you call me a
liar! You are a very bad white man—a threat to our country
and to me personally. We don't want a foreign imperialist like
yourself in Zaire. We have an effective way of dealing with a
man like you."

Things were getting worse by the minute.

"No, *Monsieur le commissaire,*" I countered, "you are not
a liar. You are only misinformed. You were not present
during the conference, and you don't really know what was
said. These accusations are lies, and I invite you to hear the
tapes."

Beads of sweat began to appear on the official's handsome ebony face. The large blood vessel in his neck was pulsating rapidly and his breath was coming in short pants. The two-toned toe of his costly high-heeled shoe (shoes that would cost a common laborer more than two months' salary) was bouncing in a staccato rhythm on the elephant-grass mat. He was mad. And I was scared.

In the tension of the moment, however, the Holy Spirit's radar continued its beeping. "What about the Order of the Leopard? Didn't the apostle Paul use his Roman citizenship in just such a tight spot?" With Spirit-inspired composure I continued my defense.

"*Monsieur le commissaire,* I am a friend of the Zairians. I came to your country long ago as a missionary to help your people in both their spiritual and their physical needs. I have spent the greatest part of my life in this area and I have many friends among your people.

"Furthermore," I ventured, "if I am as bad a man as you accuse me of being, then why did your president, *Citoyen Sese-Seko-Mobutu,* single me out to receive the highest honor of your country, the Order of the Leopard?"

Sweat began to run in rivulets down his face. The massive toe of his shiny shoe froze in midair. His jaw fell open and his eyes popped out at me in disbelief and surprise.

"Oh, Monsieur Brashler!" he ejaculated. "Congratulations! I had heard that a missionary in the province had received the distinguished honor of the Leopard, but I had no idea it was you. Now I want you to know that I am not accusing you. Some very bad people have brought me these charges, and I want to find out the truth so that I can protect you."

Actually, he was trying to protect himself; he could have gotten into serious trouble by arresting the holder of this medal. Just a few days before my confrontation with this commissaire, General Lundula, at the order of the president, had conferred this distinction on three blacks and myself.

It is a rare honor bestowed on some of the high-ranking Zairian officials and on only a very few foreigners. The moon-invading astronauts, while official visitors of President Mobutu, were thus honored—as was U.S. Ambassador Sheldon Vance, after sixteen years of heading the American Embassy in Kinshasa (formerly Léopoldville).

The honor carries with it a number of privileges, one of which is immunity to arrest. Should the holder of the Leopard be accused of a crime or a misdemeanor, he would be sent to Kinshasa to appear before the president and have his case reviewed. Should there be evidence of guilt, the president would then demote him by stripping from him the medal along with any other insignia and certificates. Then he would be turned over to the Justice Department.

Only recently Edythe had remarked, "I wonder why the Lord has allowed you to receive this distinction, and just how it will bring glory to his name." I too had wondered. On that crucial morning at Blukwa, however, I was beginning to see his purpose in it. The confrontation was over.

Since that time, this commissaire has become a good friend of ours. He has visited us in our home, and on many occasions he has been most helpful. "After all," he would frequently remark, "aren't you missionaries our friends, and here to help us?" He calls me citoyen, the French word for "citizen." It is a title the people use among themselves. They address foreigners as monsieur, except those whom they wish to pay a real compliment.

It was thus that the enemy of men's souls and of God's redemptive purposes almost succeeded in cutting off Edythe's and my missionary career ignominiously and prematurely. That career had begun in our Biola days, in the late thirties. In the following pages, the Leopard tells his story.

TWO
ARE
MISSIONARIES
FREAKS?

"Hey kids, come and look at the missionaries!" That exclamation came from a pastor as we drove up to his parsonage. We were to have a weekend of meetings in his church.

"Look, there they come! Pete and Edythe. They've just come back from Zaire. They're missionaries!" That remark was heard in the Everett (Washington) Civic Auditorium where we had come to hear Merv Rosell during a furlough.

"Here comes that confounded missionary again!" We also heard that response as we drove up to a certain home during our latest furlough.

"Pretty spiffy for a missionary!" That comment came from a godly old pastor as we appeared in a new station wagon just prior to going back for another term of service. This car would serve us for five years over the worst of roads, and where proper maintenance service is nonexistent.

Epithets and kibitzing remarks such as those are commonplace to missionaries. They learn to shrug them off. Their children, however, resent them bitterly, and often become rebellious because of them. One of the biggest problems for an M.K. (missionary kid) is to be accepted as an ordinary human being, rather than as a freak.

The popular missionary stereotypes tend to make people regard missionaries either as much holier than they really are, or as rogues. Some people, when a missionary appears,

19

snuff out their cigarette and don their spirituality cloak. Others lay a protecting hand over their wallet.

A story is told of a mother riding on a bus with her little boy. The youngster swallowed a dime and began to choke. The mother was frantic, but a fellow passenger stepped up, turned the boy upside down, shook him vigorously, and pummeled his backside until he coughed up the dime.

"Oh, doctor," exclaimed the relieved mother, "thank you so much! You knew just what to do."

"Oh, that's OK," said the stranger, "but I'm not a doctor."

"Not a doctor? Well, what are you?" demanded the woman. "You certainly knew how to get the dime out of him."

"Oh, I'm a missionary," explained the hero.

And missionaries Edythe and I are. Often the butt of a joke, often the center of a church controversy. ("What! Another offering for those missionaries? What about the dollar I gave for them at last year's missionary conference? Haven't they got those heathen converted yet?")

Frequently missionaries are a special target of Satan. There's no length to which he will not go to stymie them, especially the new ones. Often they are totally disillusioned when they arrive on the field and find that their fellow missionaries are mere men and women, people with normal capacity for making mistakes.

When we first went to the field, our general secretary warned us, "Your biggest problem will be to relate harmoniously to your fellow missionaries." Wow! That can't apply to missionaries. What about their spirituality? What about their halo? But we soon found out that our general secretary was right. Missionaries are very ordinary and very human. It's just that everything they do is magnified out of proportion.

In the light of all that, it is natural for a young man or woman to resist the missionary call. It is natural, but not spiritual. We thank God that the epithets, the kibitzers, and the attractions of America did not win out, even if we were on our way to becoming "missionary freaks."

It all started back in the "predeterminate councils" of God. (We believe in the Calvinistic, or rather the Pauline, doctrine of God's sovereignty and in his foreordained plan for our lives.) But in a contemporary sense it began in New Mexico.

My parents had moved as newlyweds from South Holland, Illinois, to the arid state of New Mexico early in this century. There were indications of tuberculosis in Dad's family so, at the strong advice of their family doctor, the whole clan moved southward. They homesteaded a 640-acre section of land, of which Dad and Mother acquired 160 acres for themselves. They started to raise not only alfalfa, but also a family —which would include, in due course, three sons and two daughters. I was born in 1912 and christened Peter James. Such a "handle" bugged me during my school days, but it managed to stick with me.

When I was about four, my parents decided to migrate to the Northwest, where my mother's family had already settled in. The health of the Brashler clan had improved sufficiently by then for them to brave the moisture of the Puget Sound climate.

My family's Dutch heritage had provided my parents with a strong allegiance to the Christian Reformed Church. But there was no such church in Arlington, Washington, the dairy-farming community to which they had gravitated. However, since religion was woven into their warp and woof, they began to visit some of the local churches.

There was a group of Plymouth Brethren there who were very spiritual, but also a bit odd. Tobacco! Whoever heard of a Christian using that stuff? If smoking were in God's plan for his children, wouldn't he have equipped the human anatomy with a smokestack? What's more, these Brethren had no ordained minister. The *dominie* (pastor) was a cultural necessity in the life of the Christian Reformers, and they gave him a very lofty place in the community. How could they ever get along without the *dominie*?

But the Brethren had something else that drew the newcomers back to the gospel hall again and again: a clear and forceful way of presenting the gospel of Christ. After exposure to such preaching, it wasn't long before Dad knew that he must make a decision or be lost forever.

One morning in the spring of 1921, as he was plowing beautiful straight furrows in the mulchy soil with his new

John Deere tractor, his spiritual battle reached a climax. He stopped the tractor and knelt in the moist furrow to surrender to the Lord. Then, with joy and exhilaration such as he had never known before, he bounded through the plowed field all the way to the farmhouse.

Mother saw him coming and was alarmed. What was wrong with her husband that he had left the shiny new tractor idling in the field? Was he sick?

"Will, what's wrong?"

"Wrong?" shouted Dad. "Not a thing in the world is wrong. Everything is 100 percent all right. I am saved! And you'd better be too, or you will be lost."

So it was that both entered into a lasting and loving relationship with their Lord. They had always been lovers, but now there was a new dimension of tenderness and meaning to their relationship.

That night we returned to the gospel hall, where another evangelist was conducting evening meetings. (The whole family was expected to go to the meetings each night, regardless of the fact that they had been up since five a.m. to do the chores.) Mother and Dad's newfound joy was shared with the company of believers; and there was great rejoicing that this handsome pair had now surrendered to Christ.

I personally resisted the urge to become a "born-again believer" for some months. Even as a nine-year-old, I became quite adroit in evading embarrassing questions and stalling off a definite commitment. But in January 1922 another Irish preacher arrived.

I did not like this evangelist. In fact, I was scared stiff of him. He had a way of ferreting out the secret sins of my heart and seeing through my deceit. The meetings were a family "must," however, and each of us kids was expected to go along and to stay awake. I doodled in the hymnbooks and, when far enough away from my parents, carved on the bench backs.

Frequently I would steal a glance at the clock on the back wall. It was a mammoth wall clock with a huge pendulum swinging back and forth, ticking off the seconds. Each tick was bringing us a step nearer to eternity, and each tock was a reminder that we should stop and do something about it. But the tick and the tock were not enough. On the door that covered the pendulum there was a motto: "Time ends, then ETERNITY."

My furtive glances at the clock did not escape the piercing eye of the preacher. His voice thundered through the gospel hall, ringing out the wrath of God—and the sure doom of a nine-year-old who had the temerity to glance at the clock, no matter how long it had been since his head had touched a pillow.

"Never mind the clock!" roared the preacher, "there'll be no clocks in hell!"

How long could a boy resist such a barrage of hell-fire preaching? More out of fear than out of a real desire for God, I received the Lord as my Savior. Modern psychology deplores such a fear motive, but in my case it worked. I knew I was a Christian, and I asked to be baptized.

"You are too young," replied the preacher. "You must wait for three years."

Not too young to go to hell for stealing a glimpse at the clock, but too young to be baptized. Stern as those Brethren were, I still have a soft spot in my heart for them. They gave me a solid footing in doctrinal truth and taught me lessons in discipline that were to pay dividends in years ahead on the mission field. Though it's over five and a half decades since that particular chapter of my life's story was written, there has never been a real doubt in my mind concerning my conversion. The Irish preacher's clincher from the Word of God has held tight. "He that believeth on the Son hath everlasting life: and he that believeth not the Son shall not see life; but the wrath of God abideth on him" (Jn. 3:36).

Elementary and high school days slipped by. At home the Bible was read twice daily in family devotions, and we were taught to pray. Work was always more than plentiful, but life was good to this Christian dairy-farming family.

There was no question but that I, too, would be a farmer. School did not interest me; the Guernsey and Jersey cows held far more attractions. Dad's retail milk business intrigued me. This was the life for me, and it was so important that I dropped out of high school in my senior year. Not until some years later did I go back to pick up those few remaining high school credits, and graduate.

With the Depression came the necessity of finding some kind of work to supplement the family income. A kindly Christian meat packer with whom Dad had done business for years, Ben Westmoreland, gave me a job in the grocery department of his large retail market. After starting as a delivery boy and working as a clerk, I was eventually given the responsibility of managing the grocery store.

Things were getting tougher on the farm, Dad had a good chance to sell, so we moved to Everett, Washington, and began attending the First Baptist Church. The pastor was another Irish preacher, Dr. H. R. McKee. This one not only preached the same gospel that the Brethren did, with the same type of Irish wit and fervor; but he also had a choir and in the choir he had a daughter, a mischievous young woman who was in due course to captivate my heart. Her name was Edythe.

During my days as a grocer I developed a habit that the Brethren had deplored: smoking. At first I smoked not because of the enjoyment it afforded, but as a means of convincing myself and others that I was a man (the down on my chin was totally inadequate). I eventually got hooked, however, and soon found it very hard to get along without frequent cigarettes.

That habit became a problem. I knew what it was doing to my body, and that it was an offense to the Holy Spirit by whom I was indwelt. One Sunday night Pastor McKee preached a sermon on consecration that convicted me even more. At the invitation I went forward to dedicate my life and to surrender my pack of Lucky Strikes. A sense of elation came over my soul as I took that step—not only to quit smoking, but also to surrender my life totally to God.

The next morning it was back to the grocery store. The thought of that comforting habit began to bother me, especially when customers came in and blew smoke in my face. Temptation? No, I had made a resolve. But, like it or not, the going was tough. I was nervous. I goofed up accounts. I was crotchety with some of our best customers. I chewed gum

24

until my jaws ached. But I did not smoke all that Monday. Tuesday morning, back to the job, and still no smokes. But when the avuncular, and normally jovial, Ben Westmoreland arrived, I was called into his office. He had a number of my accounts on his desk which he shoved toward me. "What's all this about, Pete? Why all these mistakes? This is not your kind of work. What's wrong?"

There I stood, in all my importance as manager of the little grocery store, being called on the carpet. My nicotine-stained fingers began to tremble. Sweat stood out in beads on my forehead. My eyes would not focus on the boss's big clear ones, hidden behind their horn-rimmed spectacles. I was ashamed and embarrassed. Further, I was mad.

What about this "surrender-all" business? Where was the enabling power of the Holy Spirit that the preacher had talked about so eloquently? I fidgeted. If only I could sneak out for a few minutes to light up a cigarette to relieve my frayed nerves and to regain some composure. I didn't know what to say to this boss whom I had learned to respect as a second father.

Then, with uncanny insight, Mr. Westmoreland asked me quietly, "Pete, did you smoke yesterday? Are you trying to shake that habit?" I muttered a faint affirmative. With a bound, he leaped to the floor and placed a heavy hand on my shoulder. "Pete, you go ahead and make all the mistakes you must, but don't go back to your pack! I will check your work, and make corrections. And what's more, I will be praying for you." In modern parlance he would have said, "Hang in there, Pete."

That was a crucial moment in my life, and Mr. Westmoreland sensed its importance. Had he reproached me in any way, I'm sure I would have gone straight out of the office and bought another pack of Lucky Strikes.

No more smokes. Deliverance from that habit was a big factor in setting me on the trail of becoming a missionary freak. As a result of that experience, in later years—as Africa Inland Mission field director over some 125 missionaries in Zaire, and in dealing with missionary candidates—the Lord gave me tolerance and patience when similar problems arose.

THREE
BIOLA
ROMANCE

As time went on, Edythe became more and more important to me. There had always been plenty of girls to fill dates and social occasions, and at first the Irish preacher's daughter entered my life as just another one. But after a date at the skating rink, and a number of church parties and picnics, I began to take notice of Edythe as an individual quite different. Her dad's sense of humor had rubbed off on her; there was never a dull moment when she was along.

One day Edythe invited me to join the choir. I'm sure the choir director must have thought I got my musical dexterity at Sing Sing: always behind a few bars and never quite able to get the right key. Somehow I could never seem to get beyond the "Trouble Cliff." I got through a few practices and Sunday morning performances by opening my mouth wide and mastering the proper gestures, always keeping the volume down to near zero. But the venture afforded me more time to be with Edythe—enough time, in fact, to fall in love with her.

Then, before long, Edythe decided she wanted to go to Biola (the Bible Institute of Los Angeles). Her farewell Sunday came all too soon. At the reception her father remarked, "Edythe is going to be a missionary."

"Oh, yeah?" thought I. "Not if I can help it. If she's going to be a missionary, then I'm going to step out of her life."

I wasn't happy about her even going to Biola, let alone to a foreign country. Education was fine—but why Bible school?

I later learned that Edythe also entertained some negative thoughts about being a missionary. She wanted to go to Biola, but not to the mission field, and certainly not to Africa. At least we were partially on the same wavelength.

Work in the grocery store, and life at church, were far more dull without Edythe. But life went on, and work and responsibility largely crowded out the loneliness. Happily, before we had time for too much pining, Christmas was at hand, and Edythe came home for two wonderful and warmhearted weeks.

The reunion was all we had hoped it would be, and inwardly convinced us both that we were meant for each other. We spent considerable time talking and praying about my future, as I had become convinced that I, too, should continue my interrupted studies.

"Why not come to Biola?"

"Biola? Not for me! That's final."

"Well, then, how about a visit during Easter vacation?"

A visit? Fine. In fact, that would be great, since I had never been to Southern California. We dreamed, we planned, and we decided tentatively. We would pray some more about it. It would have been much easier for me to firm up the decision then and there, but Edythe insisted that we keep on praying about it. (That practice has stuck with her, and even in the very ordinary things of life she has taught me the value of it.)

Pray about the trip we did, and Easter came quickly. The visit was a tremendous success. I ran out of money far too soon, but that did not cramp our style in those Depression days. The week was packed full of delightful experiences. I met Mr. Hale, dean of men, who was to make a lasting impression on my life. I left Biola with quite a different attitude, realizing that this was a school of both spiritual stature and academic significance. I promised Edythe that I would be praying about my own attendance there.

In September I entered Biola. Mr. Hale remembered me, which was flattering. The Lord provided work at Clifton's Restaurant at 25¢ an hour plus free meals. After a few weeks I landed a second job at the information desk, which took care of room rent. Philippians 4:19 was already beginning to become real for me.

People like Drs. Paul Rood, Elbert McCreery, Louis Talbot, Samuel Sutherland, John Hubbard, and others inspired me greatly. Not only were they mature Christians and devoted leaders; they were friendly. Access to their desk was easy. Counseling and prayer sessions with them became routine. The years at Biola passed quickly.

In the meantime my rebellion regarding the mission field persisted. What was I to do with my life? What was I to *be*? A missionary? Never. A pastor? Perhaps. A Christian businessman? A Christian farmer? One of the latter two, more than likely. Or so I thought.

But God had a plan for Edythe and me. Ralph Davis, home director of the Africa Inland Mission, spoke at Biola's missionary conference during our final year there. That remarkable man portrayed the needy mission field in central Africa so vividly and so dramatically that both of us sat up and took notice. Our good friends, Bob and Ella Deans—Plymouth Brethren M.K.s from Zaire (then Congo)—complemented Ralph Davis's messages, crossing every *t* and dotting every *i*.

The conference resulted in heart-searching times. A personal question now confronted us: What were we going to do about the needs of central Africa? It was the Holy Spirit speaking to us. There was no peace until we surrendered to the call, agreeing to accept that challenge. Gone were my dreams of the Christian farmer who would some day be wealthy enough to support God's work.

Edythe and I had not yet talked about marriage. We applied to the A.I.M. independently, each in our hearts leaving the matter of an engagement contingent on our both being accepted. After our graduation from Biola, Dr. John Hubbard —then chairman of the A.I.M. Los Angeles committee— called us into his office to announce that we had both been accepted.

"Enough said," he remarked, as he gazed at the undecorated ring finger on Edythe's left hand. I took the hint and went directly on a shopping errand at the jeweler's store at 6th and Hope Streets.

After graduation I went with about six others to Dr. Elbert McCreery's ranch in Estes Park, Colorado. Dr. McCreery was one of the original minds behind the Wycliffe movement. His health was poor at that time; so instead of going to teach at the Summer Institute of Linguistics, he invited a few students to his ranch for the same course. The summer there provided an invaluable foundation for future language study, of which we were to have a considerable amount. From this veteran missionary we also learned many lessons, spiritual and practical, that would help us cope with the problems we would encounter later in Zaire.

The problem of funds and monthly support loomed as an impossible hurdle to our going overseas. We were members of Bethel Baptist Church in Everett, a group affiliated with the Baptist General Conference. That denomination, the former Swedish Baptist Conference, had a mission program of their own. Although they knew nothing about the Africa Inland Mission or any other interdenominational boards, they somehow felt they were to be shunned. Some of the fine old Swedish pastors pleaded with me to forget about A.I.M. and to go out under the Baptist General Conference. The denomination would care for us properly, and had a good retirement program.

Those men were sincere, looking out for our good. Yet, however appealing their offer, the call to Zaire persisted. The General Conference had no work there. Our home church assured us our support, regardless of what board we went out under.

My ex-employer's wife, Esther Westmoreland, was chairwoman of the Missionary Committee and a first-class organizer. One Sunday morning she appeared in an unusually chic hat and stylish suit, carrying a huge facsimile of a calendar month with 31 numbers in place and *Pete and Edythe* in bold letters across the top. In the first four numbers she had written her own and her husband's names.

"This," she explained to the congregation, "means that my husband and I are assuming responsibility to provide financial support and to pray especially for Pete and Edythe these days. Now there remain 27 days to be filled in, and we are inviting individuals to write their names in one or more of the squares." Soon our support was pledged, and the necessary funds for departure were in hand.

The Africa Inland Mission has a strong policy against the

solicitation of funds by missionaries. Mrs. Westmoreland and the members of her committee, however, chose to do that on our behalf. Bethel Church has been our main source of financial support ever since, although several other churches in the Northwest have joined hands in this missionary venture.

By September 1939 we were itching to go to Africa, and we wanted to get married. The board had had experience with accepted candidates getting married, and then pregnancy preventing their departure, so they took no chances with us. We were to shake out the wedding confetti on the gangplank and be out to sea before such a thing could happen.

We were married on September 15. But before we could actually get aboard ship, World War II was seriously underway. Our bookings were cancelled, and we would have to wait indefinitely, it seemed.

At that time the First Baptist Church of Lake Stevens, also a General Conference church, was without a pastor. They extended us a call, and we began a double honeymoon—one our own, and the second with this church. We loved both honeymoons, so much so that when a new booking was procured six months later, I was reluctant to leave our life at Lake Stevens. But Edythe wasn't pregnant, and there were no plausible reasons why we shouldn't go.

The farewells and departure were terribly difficult. In saying goodbye, we realized how much our friends at Bethel and Lake Stevens meant to us. To this day, thirty-six years after that first farewell, such separations still bring a pain to the pit of my stomach. One of the blessings of heaven will be that to sing that tear-jerker, "God Be With You Till We Meet Again," will no longer be necessary.

FOUR
MISSIONARY
BEGINNINGS

The sheet was wringing wet. Sweat formed in droplets on Edythe's face and lips. She was perspiring profusely and her temperature registered over 103 degrees; but at the same time she was chilled to the bone. Her limbs felt as if they were going to break off at the sockets. Her head felt like a hippo's —only a hippo-sized skull could be big enough for such a headache. It was then that I began to appreciate what a winner I had received at the marriage altar. She was thoroughly miserable, yet what a brave front she managed.

But what was wrong with her? Was it pregnancy? No other pregnant women we knew of had ever had symptoms such as these. This was different, and it was alarming. But old Mother Propst, hostess at the mission's Mayfield Guest House in Nairobi, Kenya, was reassuring. She diagnosed it immediately and accurately as malaria. Didn't she know the symptoms and hadn't she had such attacks many times herself?

She called the doctor, who happened to be in Nairobi from Kijabe. This old veteran prescribed quinine, the most effective malarial treatment known in 1940. The treatment was drastic, almost as drastic as the disease itself. It made one's ears buzz like a buzz saw and sooner or later affected one's hearing. (It was for this reason that so many of the old-timers wore those awkward and conspicuous hearing aids.) But it was the only treatment to be had.

The dosage was to be repeated for three days. Soon the fever was down, but Edythe still felt miserable and had to stay in bed for a number of days.

The experience discouraged us totally. We thought about our families and friends at Bethel and the Lake Stevens church. The partings had been so bittersweet—so many expressions of love and kindness. In our distress the memories clung to us with nostalgic tenderness. Did we do right in coming to Africa? Couldn't we have done a greater work in Lake Stevens? Would we ever see our loved ones again? What was this we had heard about blackwater fever resulting from serious attacks of malaria and the malarial treatment?

Doldrums. Self-pity. Right down into their depths we plunged. What if I should lose my bride in such an attack? Yet we couldn't turn around and go back now. What would our friends say? Maybe we should finish our first term in the shortest time possible and then go home. Neither the Lord nor our friends would expect more of us than that.

We had been too busy all along to get down to the business of serious prayer. Biola days had been far too fast-paced. In those delightful but hectic pastoral pursuits at Lake Stevens there was never enough time. The frenetic activity prior to our leaving was also too full for anything but perfunctory prayer. The Lord knew we needed training in this area. How could we engage in spiritual warfare unless we became much more than amateurs in this basic stratagem?

We had some hard lessons to learn, and we are still amazed at the tender and loving way that the Lord went about teaching us.

At Kijabe, the largest A.I.M. station (and incidentally, the largest mission station in the world), lived an old pioneer missionary. He was affectionately known to the mission family as Father Downing. During the two weeks we were held up because of Edythe's illness we were guests in his home. This bachelor missionary had lost his wife some years before. Now he immediately recognized our situation and took us on as his project.

Father Lee Downing had spent his adult life on the mission field, working as an evangelist, pastor, counselor, and for many years as Kenya field director. He was weather-worn, wizened, and wonderful. After our first breakfast with him, with the aroma of Kenya coffee and bacon and eggs still permeating the air, he read to us. "Cast not away therefore your confidence.... For ye have need of patience, that, after ye have done the will of God, ye might receive the promise. For yet a little while, and he that shall come will come, and will not tarry" (Heb. 10:35-37).

We sat in the breakfast room for several hours, unaware of the ticking of the old grandfather clock, while this man of God shared with us the pathos, romance, and sheer happiness of his missionary experiences. He and his wife had learned about not casting away their confidence, about their need of patience. Now he was teaching us.

Our doldrums were banished. That post-breakfast session with Father Downing became a pattern for us during our two-week stay, and the inspiration of those mornings has never been forgotten. Talk about an orientation class for our work ahead—this one was unsurpassable.

Our mountaintop experience ended all too quickly, and it was time to go on to Congo. The train trip over the Kenya plains was great. Vast herds of gazelles, zebras, and giraffes grazed along the tracks as the little engine labored up the hills and puffed through the valleys. Periodically it had to stop to take on more firewood. Begging urchins appeared at the train windows at every stop, scrambling madly and getting embroiled in fist fights to get the coins thrown out by passengers. What a mission field! Could Congo be like this?

We soon found the answer to that question. After several nights on the toiling train, a boat trip over Lake Kioga, and finally another boatride down the Nile River, we reached Rhino Camp, Uganda, where the Congo field director met us and drove us the remainder of the journey over the stony road.

Crossing the Congo border was a thrill. Bill Pontier, a missionary at the border town of Aru, was there to meet us. He ran interference for us and got us through the press of immigration and customs. The sounds that issued from some of those fat Belgian officials were intriguing. I was surprised to hear Mr. Pontier use quite a different language from the French that I was expecting. It turned out to be Flemish.

At the mission station, I was further intrigued—not to

mention embarrassed. The Lugbara Christian women had gathered together on the front veranda of the Pontier home to meet the new missionaries, and immediately Edythe and I found ourselves in the midst of some forty bronzed and bare-breasted women. I frantically searched for an escape.

"But no!" I was told, "the women want to meet you, the new *bwana* as well as the new *madame*, and they want to shake your hand."

As I shook hands with the women, I did not know where to look. I tried focusing my eyes on the missionary hostess, but in so doing I stumbled into one of the black women's arms. These women were lovely, totally unaffected by my embarrassment. Their skins gleamed with the palm oil that had been rubbed on them. Colorful bands of beads hung gracefully about their hips, with bunches of fresh crisp manioc leaves tucked in front and in back. Their hair was tightly braided in typical Bantu style. Relaxed and jovial, they wanted to welcome us as their new teachers. I came to appreciate them as sisters in the Lord, but it took awhile.

Right then, I was relieved to get off that grass-thatched veranda and out into the courtyard with a group of men, each of whom wore a shirt and shorts. Many sported hats at rakish angles. Some wore shoes totally beyond repair, and seldom matched. Nearly all had a walking cane: the symbol of authority for the chief and the elders, but a symbol of sophistication for others. I learned later that we westerners look just as unusual to Africans.

They had a different smell about them, too. In 1940 a jar of Mum deodorant was a must for Americans. We wouldn't think of going out without that protection. But to Africans our Mum smell, we learned, was offensive, as were our perfumed talcs and shaving lotions. Because we were their brothers and sisters in the Lord, they graciously put up with our smells and annoying ways. But they prayed that we would soon be like them, even to the point that we would smell like them and eat and sleep as they did. They wanted us to identify with them, and we learned that identification was a must if we were ever going to be effective missionaries.

Our first six months were spent at Adja with Harold and Jane Amstutz. They were young, having arrived just three years earlier. And they were adept in practical skills, both in the kitchen and workshop. Each day Mrs. Amstutz gave us a long lesson in Bangala, the trade language, and each afternoon I worked in the carpenter's shop. There I learned to shape up some of the basic furniture we would need, practicing Bangala phrases we had learned that morning.

The days with the Amstutzes were enjoyable and gratifying. The language lessons were a delight, and we made good progress. Of course, one does not learn an African language in six months, or even six years. There are so many new words and phrases to memorize. But the language barrier was not nearly so formidable to us as we had believed it would be. Rather, it was a challenge, and not without its humor.

Edythe had worked hard on her lessons and had passed her first exam, part of which was to give a brief message to the African women. That hurdle cleared, she was ready to take on a hygiene class with the women.

One habit the women had was somewhat frightening. Inside the beaded belt she wore, each woman carried a little utility knife. That piece of equipment was used for cutting vegetables, peeling sweet potatoes or manioc roots, digging out infected chiggers from under the toenails, or picking the teeth. But the thing that most worried Edythe was to see them use this miniature knife to dig wax out of their ears. She was sure they would pierce their eardrums.

The name for such a knife in Bangala is *mbeli*. Edythe warned them constantly against the use of the *mbeli* inside their ears. On one occasion, after another such warning, there was uncontrollable laughter. "Some goof I've made," thought Edythe, "but what?" Not until after talking it over with Mrs. Amstutz did she realize her mistake. Another word in Bangala is similar to *mbeli*, but with a slight change in the first syllable. She had told them not to clean their ears with their *mabeli* instead of *mbeli*. The word *mabeli* means "breast."

One of the most enjoyable sports for our Zairian friends is to get together in a group where a ham will mimic the missionary—either in his use of the language, his manner of walk, or the way he preaches. We provided them with many laughs.

FIVE
ROOTED
AND UPROOTED

Life at Adja with the Amstutzes was by no means problem-free. We went to Africa under the illusion that we loved the Africans, and we were ready to live a life of sacrifice because of our love for them. It wasn't long, however, before that romantic dream blew up in our faces.

We learned soon enough that the blacks did not always appreciate our love for them, nor the sacrifices we were making for them. We had heard that they always had great respect for missionaries, but we soon found ourselves in culture shock. The blacks had a selfhood all their own, and they were not about to be poured into the white man's mold. Disillusionment, disappointment, and disenchantment set in, almost to the point of total discouragement.

Our love for our African friends began to cool, and we often displayed signs of irritation with them. Our spiritual glow was giving way to gloom. The deep love we thought we had for the Africans would at times disappear completely. Where now was the halo we had so piously worn back there in Everett? We were so helplessly human. How could God use us?

But as we prayed more earnestly, we again began to "taste and see" the goodness of God. Lessons learned from Father Downing flashed back to mind. "Cast not away therefore your confidence." "Ye have need of patience." We read again our mandate: "All authority is given unto me in heaven and on earth," said our Lord. "Go ye therefore. . . ."

The Lord dealt with us patiently and tenderly. He caused us to see that he had every right to send us to Africa and to put us in a difficult spot. His authority over us was absolute. Hadn't he died for our sins? Wasn't the Apostle Paul himself a "bondslave of Jesus Christ"?

With that glimpse of our Lord's glory, our circumstances took on a different perspective. Our being at Adja had nothing to do with our love for the Africans. Often they were unlovely; but so were we—no doubt more so. With a fresh vision of our Lord we began to reevaluate our motives. We accepted the fact that God had complete control over us, and we realized that a fresh surrender was needed.

Once again the joy of the Lord appeared. We may not have loved the Africans much at first, but we were beginning to love them. Now we were ready to throw ourselves into the work at Adja.

During that period, World War II was accelerating. Mail was not coming through, and it often took more than three months to hear from home. Gas was almost unavailable. The little reserve that the Amstutzes had was guarded carefully. There was no radio at Adja during those days, so we had no way of knowing how things in the world were going.

At that point Mr. Pontier, back at the border station of Aru, received a visitor: a bulky Belgian border official.

"Ach, Mijn Heer Pontier," exclaimed the visitor in his guttural Flemish, "why don't you place missionaries at the Adi mission station? Let me tell you something in the strictest confidence. The army is planning to take over that station very soon and turn it into a military camp. If you don't send missionaries there without delay, you will lose the station."

That bit of news was very upsetting to Mr. Pontier. Adi was one of our loveliest stations among the Kakwa tribe. It was located in the northeast corner of the country, about fifteen miles from the Uganda border and about eighteen miles from the Sudan. I was later to visit that corner and sit on a rock in Zaire, with one foot in Sudan and the other in Uganda. I prayed for all three countries as I sat there.

No missionaries had lived at Adi for nine months. There was a large boys' boarding school there, with a dormitory to sleep 150. There was also a large girls' school and a dispensary. The church at the station had more than 650 members at the time. A little bookstore under African management was selling vast numbers of Bangala New Testaments and hymnbooks, as well as tracts and other study booklets. The previous missionaries had had to leave for family reasons. Now the Belgian army wanted to take over the whole station.

This news was immediately sent to Mr. George Van Dusen at Aba, some 150 miles to the north, and an emergency field council meeting was called. What was to be done? Because of the war, no new workers had arrived in the six months since we had come. Every other station was understaffed.

A light came on in the field director's mind. What about the Brashlers? They could fill the bill. The Amstutzes would have to get along at Adja alone.

"But," argued some of the council members, "this new pair can barely speak Bangala. Think of the blunders they will make. The work is so vast at Adi, and if they make a mistake it will be a catastrophe. It will never work."

All of this was only too logical. To send a new couple into that situation was to take a big risk. But as the council continued to deliberate, it became obvious that they must take this risk. Unless they sent the Brashlers, the army would confiscate the place.

The decision was communicated to us at Adja the next day. For us it was another rending experience. We enjoyed working with the Amstutzes, and we were beginning to put down roots. We had plans for a house and had already laid the foundation. We had made good progress with Bangala; but of course, the trade language would be the same at Adi. The gravity of the situation was explained to us, but no one was asking us whether we would be willing to go. We were being told what to do and to do it immediately.

The next day Mr. Amstutz loaded us and all our household goods into his panel delivery truck. (We didn't realize how meager our belongings were until we got them into the house later.) All of our things went into that small vehicle, except for one kitchen cabinet I had made. There was no room for that, but Mr. Amstutz had the solution.

He called six of his workmen to come with three long poles. The cupboard was laid across the poles, and the three men on each side boosted the cupboard up on their heads. In their bare feet they set out over the sixty miles of gravel road. Thus our cupboard was delivered by African transfer three days later. We made the trip by car in about two hours.

Africa is beautiful in early December. As we rode in the little van, flocks of guinea fowl chattered noisily. Beautiful birds they were, and they must have looked to us like the wild turkeys did to the Pilgrim fathers. They were delicious, and could add splendor to our spartan diet. Mr. Amstutz rode on the fender with his .12-gauge shotgun, ready to shoot. He bagged several of them near Adi, but he continued to ride outside until we got to the station.

No cars except army vehicles had driven into Adi for a number of weeks. Soldiers were the only guests the Africans had seen for a long time. Whenever a car came toward Adi the signal was passed from village to village by the African telegraphic system. We were still miles away from the station when the signal came through. Africans gathered along the road in great excitement. *Masua azali kuyia* (A car is arriving).

Once they saw us, their euphoria gave way to fear. Mr. Amstutz was still perched on the fender with his gun under his arm. This was wartime in Europe, and its effects did not escape even this isolated corner of Africa. A truck with a khaki-clad man with gun in hand certainly meant trouble. Perhaps they would be driven out of their homes, and many would be killed. Instead of the enthusiastic cry of welcome that was customary when a missionary or a friendly Belgian official drove up, there was stark fear. The crowds stood frozen in terror as we drove up to the big mission house.

As soon as they recognized Mr. Amstutz, there was a shout of hilarious welcome. Hundreds of schoolchildren started their welcome march, beating their drums and chanting their rhythmic songs. The boys were followed by a large group of young women from the girls' school. Their crisp, green leaf skirts swished from side to side in perfect rhythm. I was no longer embarrassed at the sight of bare breasts.

Mothers followed, babies strapped piggyback style, with heads dangling from side to side as the women pressed toward the car. When a baby began to cry, it was deftly taken from its perch, passed under the mother's arm, and set to nursing. Still, the babies looked so undernourished. The men were there too. These men and women had been working hard in their gardens, and there was the rancid smell of sweat.

Finally the pastor and seven dignified church elders approached us. We were introduced to them as the new missionaries from Adja who had arrived six months earlier. They had heard of us, and their joy knew no limits when they were told that we had now been assigned to Adi. At least they were going to have missionaries to work with them again. The elders and Pastor Yoane Akudri shook our hands warmly. All the old men, lined up in rows, waited for us to pass by them and shake their hands. Then came the women, the schoolboys, the schoolgirls.

We pressed literally thousands of hands that afternoon. Some were calloused and gnarled from work. Some were those of an artist, with long tapered fingers. Some were grimy from garden work. Most showed signs of *panda*, a stubborn and contagious itch. Some were deformed because of the infected chiggers that nested under the nails. A few were wasted away by leprosy.

We saw those outstretched hands not only as an expression of their desire to greet us, but as a symbol of outreached hands everywhere. Hands reaching out for something that would meet their spiritual as well as physical needs. The words of Jeremiah came to us. "Is it nothing to you, all ye that pass by? behold, and see if there be any sorrow like unto my sorrow . . ." (Lam. 1:12).

As we made our way through the enthusiastic crowd, our hearts were gladdened. These were the people whom we had now come to serve. The big old brick house with the thatched roof was to be our home. The closely cropped lawn, several acres of it, encircled by well-trimmed English-style hedges was to be our playground. These blacks were to be our neighbors for an indefinite period. Perhaps until death. Perhaps until Christ came for us. We were in God's appointed place for as long a time as he should see fit to leave us there.

We entered the eight-room house with its large encircling veranda, and our inflated spirits went swoosh. The place was a mess. Had the church leaders been warned of our coming, they would have whitewashed the walls and varnished the floors. By then it was dark, and Mr. Amstutz had left us to go back to Adja. The smoky lantern was our only light. We were alone in this big dirty house.

A meager supper, a bath, and then it was time to prepare for the night. We assembled the bed and put up the mosquito nets. Our emotions played tricks on us that night. Sleep was slow in coming and intermittent. We talked about the crowds of people and their enthusiastic welcome. We felt the loneliness of being the only missionaries at this station, more than fifty miles away from our nearest white neighbors. We thought about Everett, Washington; our families; our friends at Bethel and Lake Stevens.

Overhead there was a persistent noise in the elephant-grass ceilings. It sounded like a dozen packs of rats on the rampage. "Let's pray that they don't come crawling down the mosquito net," we told each other. Those pests kept us awake, but God was near. Toward dawn we drifted off to sleep with Psalm 4:8 ringing in our hearts. "I will both lay me down in peace, and sleep: for thou, Lord, only makest me dwell in safety."

We learned in the morning that the invaders overhead were not rats, but termites. They were having a gourmet feast on elephant grass and ceiling joists. In fact, the morning sunlight showed us that some of the joists were completely eaten through, and might come crashing down onto the bed.

But we were ready for a new day and for whatever problems it would present.

SIX
BRICK, MORTAR, AND ANTHILL CLAY

"Go to the ant, thou sluggard; consider her ways, and be wise . . ." (Prov. 6:6). Those "ceiling ants" were relentless in doing their best to give all sluggards the lesson that Solomon had in mind.

Our first job was to send out for some straight eucalpytus poles, have them adzed into shape, and replace the whole ceiling. We found gallons of used motor oil, which we mixed with a stock disinfectant dip and applied to the ceiling poles. That gave the poles a flavor totally unpalatable to ants, so for years to come the ceilings were unmolested.

The workmen showed us where to get *pembi*, a white clay from the stream beds that was used as a whitewash. It took several days, but the improvement was amazing. The walls glistened in their snow-white coat.

The floors were a worse problem. There were large holes where white ants had made their nests. These we filled with rock and pounded smooth. The mud plaster over the top made them look like big black cakes, frosted over with chocolate frosting. But the mud would soon dry and leave large cracks all over. Mud would be a good breeding place for fleas and chiggers. Our workmen told us we would have to *pakela* all the floors. A thick coat of African varnish would have to be applied.

The *kapita* (captain) of the workmen had a group of women

march into the house. On their heads were flat woven baskets containing clean sand from the stream. Next they carried in buckets of manioc brine, which was dumped on the sand. The brine would keep the ants away. Finally the same women came in, their baskets filled with fresh cow manure this time. The smell made me homesick again for the farm; but the prospects for our house did not look too promising at this juncture.

Pailfuls of water were poured on the peculiar mound and then thoroughly mixed in. The women tramped and kneaded the stuff with their bare feet until it was like a huge pile of Cream of Wheat. Then, on their knees in this smooth varnish, the women began to plaster the floors with their bare hands. They chattered and laughed and gossiped as they worked. Finally they began to chant African songs to the rhythm of their swishing and swooshing. The mountain of varnish vanished. How they worked. Then the job was done, and the house smelled like a cow barn in the spring.

We were puzzled about the use of cow manure. That type of varnish, the Africans explained, would not allow the mud to crack. More important, it would keep fleas and chiggers out. (It would keep us out too, we feared.) The workmen threw all the windows and doors open, so that the dry-season wind could whip through the house.

Why all this fuss over white ants? One of our missionaries, we were told, had ordered a new pair of trousers from Montgomery Ward. After many months of waiting, the pants finally arrived. He wore them proudly the first day he had them, and he was the envy of the station. Such a nice new pair of khaki pants. That night as he donned his pajamas he hung the pants over a chair with the pant legs resting on the floor. Next morning he reached for the pants to wear them the second day, but they stuck to the floor. He gave them a little jerk and the pants came up but both cuffs stuck fast to the floor. They had been eaten by the white ants.

In several hours our floors were dry, and the smell not nearly so bad. By late afternoon we were beginning to move our furniture into place: a table, several folding chairs used as dining chairs, a few boxes covered with calico cloth that were to serve as cupboards for our dishes and silverware. We had a good Simmons double bed, which stood majestically in the large bedroom. It was our only piece of proper furniture, and it had proved to be a wise investment, freight costs notwithstanding. We manufactured our own stove by building a brick shell, using a wash boiler for the oven and adding a flattened-out gasoline barrel for the top. It smoked, but it cooked our meals and baked our bread.

The long process of gathering furniture and making the house more comfortable and attractive had begun. Edythe proved to be skillful in turning any wooden box or packing crate into an attractive piece of furniture. The house was soon home to us. The Africans came in constant groups for a guided tour through the *mondeli's* (white man's) house.

Not long after our arrival at Adi we were called on by a delegation, including Pastor Yoane Akudri, the seven elders of the church, and some of the workmen. They had a problem they wanted to share with us, but in typical Bantu fashion they talked about many things before they actually broached the subject of their errand.

"Bwana," the pastor began, "we have seen how you have fixed up your house, and we think it is very nice. We are happy with you that you have such a luxurious place to live. This must surely please God, as it does us."

All of this I recognized as preliminary, a means of preparing the way for the real problem. Finally it was out. "Bwana," continued the pastor, "don't you think it would please the Lord if we had a lovely new church building, like Mr. Amstutz is building at Adja? We have several thousand people attending our services every Sunday, and we need a new church building. We want you to help us."

We had heard that in many cases African churches expected help from overseas to finance such projects. They also expected the missionary to pay for lumber, glass, roofing, doors, windows, etc., and to provide a truck for the transport of the materials. The mission had no money for this building, and it was certain that from our scant allowance Edythe and I would be able to help very little. How was I to answer this request? I did not want to offend, nor did I want to offer false hope. "Lord, help me to answer this request," I prayed silently.

As the delegation sat and fidgeted, waiting for my answer, I could see that their desire for a new church was real. I also knew that it was impossible for me to help them. I was no builder, nor was I a financier. In my most diplomatic manner I started to give them my realistic opinion.

"My dear brothers, your desire for a new church building is good. This would bring glory to God. I know there are crowds that attend on Sunday who cannot get inside the old chapel for lack of room. You must have a new church, but have you thought of these factors? First, you will need more than a million bricks to build a church of adequate size. Then you will need more than 25,000 tiles to cover the roof. Also, you will need several thousand feet of lumber for the job, as well as money enough to pay salaries for masons, carpenters, and sawyers. All this will take lots of money—at least 50,000 francs."

I was pulling the figures off the top of my head, but I had listened to Mr. Amstutz discuss these things. It sounded as though I spoke with authority. In any case, I wanted the figures to be on the generous side rather than skimpy.

"Further," I continued, "you must realize that the mission has no money to help finance the project. Nor do we have much extra personal money that we can put into it. Nor am I a builder who can give leadership to such a project. And we don't have a truck to transport the materials to the building site."

Certainly that speech would quash the idea of a building program. I offered one further idea. "Why don't we consider enlarging the old chapel?" That suggestion went over like a monkey in their peanut garden.

"How many bricks did you say would be needed?"

"At least a million!" I replied.

The pastor wrote something down. Then he asked for specifics regarding the number of tiles, the amount of lumber, and how much money I thought we would need. I gave what I thought were rather exaggerated answers to each of these questions. He wrote down more. I emphasized that we should certainly have the million bricks in hand, and also the 50,000 francs, before we could ever get started on the project. Further, I asked in desperation, "Whom can we get to direct this building project?" I was running scared.

They saw no problems. They would ask the capable and jovial Mr. Amstutz to draw up plans and to help with the very important work of putting in the foundation and laying the first several courses of bricks. After that there would be no problems for awhile. When they got up to the roof, they would again ask Mr. Amstutz to help them get started with the first truss. From there we would be on our own.

They were looking to me for leadership. We prayed and the delegation left.

Sleep was scant that night as I reflected on my new role as church builder. Oh well, I mused as the first roosters of the dawn began to crow, they don't have their million bricks yet, nor their 50,000 francs. I had made it clear to them that the bricks and money must be in hand before we could get started. It would be a long time before I would really have to worry about it.

How wrong can a person be? Within a week hundreds of church members were at the mission station from all over the district. Were they having a conference? "No," explained the pastor. "We will have only about three months of dry season, and we want to make the bricks for the church before the rains start."

For the next three months there were constant teams of brickmakers. The women again tramped the anthill clay into smooth mortar, which was placed in brick molds and carried out into the vast drying fields. The sun baked the bricks for a day, and then in the evening they were turned over to bake on the other side. The next day they were stood on end and the following day turned over to the opposite end. Later they were stacked up to dry thoroughly. That process went on day after day until there was a mountain of bricks. No one tried to count to see if we had the million, but certainly there were huge quantities.

Toward the end of the dry season a large area was cleared and leveled. The bricks were stacked into a long kiln, about 20 feet deep and over 100 feet long. Twenty fire boxes were arched into the kiln, and the brick stacking went on in earnest until the kiln reached high into the heavens. Several such kilns were made and then plastered over with mud.

There was great excitement when the fires were finally laid and ignited. In the dark night, the whole area was lit up by the bright red glow of the kilns. For a week they burned, until a frosty white color began to appear all over the kilns at the cracks. They had "finished to finish" explained the pastor in his colloquial Bangala. "Now," he said, "we can get started on the building."

I hemmed a bit at this observation and finally asked, "What about the 50,000 francs?"

"Oh, that?" said Yoane. "We shall come to see you at your house this evening."

They came with the money in a gunnysack, which they dumped out on our varnished floor. How much was there? They weren't certain, but they knew it was more than 50,000 francs. They would need more, so they had told the members to be ready to give additional money. Some of the women had not yet sold their millet. The men, too, would go out on another elephant hunt and sell the meat at the market. The exchequer would be kept well supplied, they assured me.

The whole project continued to prosper in just that fashion. The sawyers felled the trees and maneuvered them over large pits. With pit saws they ripped the long roof timbers into twenty-eight-foot lengths. They ripped miles of one-inch planks and cut them into four-inch laths which were to serve as cradles for the tiles. The tiles were made from the same white anthill clay that the women used for making cooking pots.

The masons, sawyers, and carpenters worked for more than three years before the job was completed. Mr. Amstutz made periodic trips to guide and to inspect. Often whole sections of masonry had to be torn out and done over, yet there was no grumbling. It was done for the glory of God.

I myself became more enthusiastic, once I saw that the building was a must and once I gained a bit of confidence. The church bore the burden of the work as well as the burden of the finances. I was just a partner in the scheme. The church building, finished in 1943, stands three and one-half decades later to the glory of God.

SEVEN
DISPENSARY
MINISTRY

"Kebukebu! I want to thank God for my *kebukebu!"*

Those words came from Doruka at the close of the Communion service, and what nonsense it was. *Kebukebu* is the Bangala word for "leprosy," and poor old Doruka's body was full of it. Where her feet had once been, there were only suppurating stubs. Her legs were full of open, running sores. Her hands were knobby fingerless stumps that gripped her long walking stick the way a pipe wrench would grip the end of a pipe. Her body was emaciated.

The doctors called hers a "burned-out" case, and nothing could be done for her. Even the new miracle drugs that had been used with such success in less advanced cases would not help Doruka. Now she was thanking God for her dreadful disease.

Leprosy has been the scourge of Africa for centuries. Thanks to new medication, it is now being controlled. The first signs of the disease are discolored spots on the skin. When these appeared, the doctor was often at a loss, not knowing whether it was leprosy or a new case of the itch. Sometimes, in order to confirm the diagnosis, the doctor surreptitiously stuck a pin into the spot. If the patient reacted in pain, the doctor knew that it wasn't leprosy. A leprosy patient is insensate to pain in the infected areas.

Doruka had once appeared at our door with legs that

showed even bloodier sores than usual. I expressed concern and asked her if her disease was getting worse.

"Oh no," she replied, "those sores are not because of my *kebukebu*. Last night as I lay sleeping, rats came in and chewed on my legs, and I was unaware of it until daylight came. Then I chased the miserable rodents away."

Now Doruka had taken her first Communion. She had a bright kerchief on her head that had been given to her by some of the other Christian women. I had baptized her that morning, along with 105 other Christians. Doruka had been the last one, lest she defile the pool. She was thrilled to be baptized, and now to receive the bread and wine for the first time. Because her fingerless hands were not able to pick up the morsel of bread, I dropped it in the palm of her hand and she deftly tossed it into her mouth. She had held the cup of juice firmly between the palms of her hands and raised it to her lips. The service was about over, when Doruka made her astounding statement about being thankful for leprosy.

"What do you mean, Doruka?" I asked. "Why are you thankful for it?"

"*Bwana,* it is because of my leprosy that I came to this mission dispensary. I thought I could receive *dawa* (medicine) that would heal my disease, but it is not helping in my advanced case. I shall die in this condition—no doubt very soon. But while I was here, I learned that I had another disease. That was the leprosy of sin. For this sickness I have received the proper *dawa*. The blood of Jesus Christ was applied for my sins.

"Today I have been baptized, and now I have taken my first Communion to remind me of the price that Jesus paid to bring healing to my soul. That is why my heart is full of thankfulness even for my *kebukebu*. It was through my sickness that I came to know the Lord."

Doruka taught me an important lesson that day. Sometimes I had regarded medical work as secondary. Today as I looked over that sea of black faces I realized for the first time that the majority of them had come into the church through the door of the dispensary.

Medical work plays a large part in the work of the Africa Inland Mission. Dr. Carl Becker, now an octogenarian, retired from the field only recently. He went to Congo to work with the mission in the late twenties. He and his wife, a schoolteacher, had a promising future before them in Boyertown, Pennsylvania. But after eleven years of medical practice there, God tapped him on the shoulder for service overseas. Although Carl was ready to give up his promising practice at once, the Boyertown Chamber of Commerce had different ideas. They wanted this young doctor to stay in their town, and they offered to pay all the expenses for two other doctors to go out as missionaries in Carl Becker's place.

But the young professional and his equally brilliant wife had orders from a higher authority. It was God who was sending them to Africa. For over forty-five years, then, they labored there, trying to treat such patients as Doruka. (Their story is told in *Another Hand On Mine* by William J. Petersen.)

There were never enough doctors and nurses to meet the colossal medical needs. The mission saw the need for training African paramedics, nurses, and midwives and gave them the best training possible—recognized and certificated by the government. Thus qualified, these women and men staffed dispensaries all through the area—one thousand miles in length, and some two hundred miles in width—for which the mission was responsible.

All of the mission stations have radio communications and can consult with the doctors at the medical center. Two small planes with Missionary Aviation Fellowship pilots stand by for emergency cases.

The mission has been criticized by some for "majoring in minors," expending so many resources on medical and educational work. Yet that first baptismal service at Adi that day had convinced me of the worth of it. Our missionary mandate includes humanitarian outreach as well as the preaching of the gospel, as is seen in Jesus' own ministry of teaching and healing. Doruka, like tens of thousands of others, would never have been brought into the church had it not been for the mission's medical ministry.

In the early years at Adi, Africans frequently came to us with intense toothaches. Often we would have to confine our assistance to an aspirin, a prayer, a "God bless you," and an explanation of the gospel. Those individuals, however, were interested in nothing but help for their aching tooth. They would beg the *infirmier* (male nurse) or the missionary to extract the menacing molar. Once that was cared for, they would listen to the gospel.

The first such occasion came to us at Adi when the *infirmier* was away. A suffering man stood before me with his little shenzi dog at his side. He had his fist pressed against his jaw, and he was in misery. *"Bwana,"* he cried, "pull my tooth! It's killing me!"

I looked at the shenzi pup, full of sores and covered with flies. The dog could not have cared less about the flies, the mange, or the sores. His soulful and empathetic expression seemed to say, "Please, my master's tooth is torturing him. Won't you pull it out?"

I had never pulled a tooth before, I told the man. Further, I had no Novocain to inject as a pain-killer.

"Never mind," he begged. "What does it matter that you have never done it before? You are a white man, and you can do anything!" I felt like running away, but where? Finally I consented to give it a try.

Dr. Russell Baird from Everett had given us an assortment of forceps, along with some elementary instruction in using them. The patient sat before me, his mouth wide open. With a chigger-infected finger, he pointed to the aching tooth. Dr. Baird had said that the points of the forceps should be forced well under and between the molar's two roots. Sweat poured from my body. My hands were trembling. I expected my patient to writhe in pain, but not so. A resolute stoic, he sat as though his head were held fast in a vice. Not a whimper.

The pulling and tugging seemed endless. Was I going to yank out this poor creature's whole jaw? There were more frenetic pulls and groans. Then the tooth gave way, and I sat down, completely unnerved.

The man spat out the salt water I had given him to rinse his mouth and grinned as he wiped off his chin. *"Merci, bwana,"* he exclaimed gratefully. "You have finished to overcome! You have pulled the toothache right out of my mouth. To-night I will sleep again."

We gave him several aspirin to make sure that he would,

and from then on he was my friend. Now he was ready to listen to what we had to say about the Savior.

Every day brought new and interesting cases. After a preaching safari, Pastor Banduni was walking back to the station through wild country. Hearing a noise behind him, he turned to see a herd of elephants coming his way. The huge beasts had not detected him, since the wind was blowing from behind. Elephants are dull of hearing and their sight is poor, but they have a keen sense of smell that enables them to track down their enemies.

The preacher scaled the nearest large tree with the skill of an athlete, thus gaining safety from the beasts below. Then, as the elephants passed the tree and got downwind, they smelled their human foe. With loud trumpetings and blowing of dust, they surrounded the tree. Even though Banduni was out of reach, the elephants lingered nearby until late in the afternoon before wandering on.

The man in the tree had sat in a cramped position for hours and was suddenly very uncomfortable. Alas, a branch broke, and down he tumbled. When things began to black out around him, he realized he was seriously hurt. His last conscious thoughts were on the elephants downwind from him. They could still come back to the tree. But he was in God's hand, he thought as he passed out.

How long Banduni was unconscious he did not know. On waking up, his first thoughts were of the elephants and of how he had called upon the Lord for protection. As he lay there he could still hear them, but he became aware of the fact that the wind had changed directions completely. Now the breeze was blowing from the direction of the beasts, and they were again oblivious of their human prey. The Lord was indeed protecting him.

The pain was excruciating and he felt nauseated. As he began to examine his wounded leg, he touched the jagged ends of large leg bones protruding through the flesh—a compound fracture. Placing a forked stick into the ground, he eased his wounded leg into the crotch.

From the stars he saw that it was still early evening. Would he survive the night? He became more aware of God's presence as he kept sniffing the wind and realizing that God was

55

keeping him on the lee side of the deadly beasts. They lingered within only a few hundred yards of him through the night, totally ignorant of his presence.

At dawn, search parties set out to hunt for the missing minister. The nearest villagers knew which trail he had planned to take. They had also heard the elephants, and were afraid that their beloved spiritual father had run afoul of the creatures. Soon after daybreak they found the wounded pastor, made a stretcher of sapling poles and elephant grass, and carried him about twenty miles to the dispensary.

Banduni's case was far too serious for the *infirmier*, so he was taken by car to the nearest hospital. At Kuluva, eighty miles away, the doctor and nurses operated on the broken limb and nursed him along for weeks. Finally gangrene set in, and amputation was necessary to save his life.

Banduni recovered quickly after the amputation. He soon learned to walk on crutches, and was getting around the wards preaching the gospel. But he felt awkward on crutches, and someone had told him about an artificial limb. Could the doctors contrive such a thing for him?

Ingeniously, the doctors carved one out of balsa wood. In time they came up with several models, and after a number of lessons and attempts, Banduni was on his feet again. In fact, he now had four legs: one his own; a second, artificial one for working in the garden; a third for riding his bicycle; and a fourth, a fancy leg with a sock and shoe laced on the foot of it, for preaching.

A bicycle was purchased for him, and he could be seen— with his broad grin—riding his bike over the trails to his preaching appointments. The bicycle leg was fastened to the stump of his own limb, and his preaching leg to the luggage rack of his bike. He would change before the service began. He was now more mobile than ever before. After that we referred to him as "the man with one foot in the grave."

EIGHT
WHAT MISSIONARIES FACE

On our way to Africa the first time there were many well-wishers to see us off—most of them gracious, but some of them tactless and overbearing. One such well-wisher said, "I have a brother in seminary. If he makes a failure of being a pastor, then we'll send him to Africa, too. You could use him there."

It has never ceased to amaze us that so many Americans think of foreign missionaries as sort of second-rate servants of God, men and women who cannot quite compete with their peers and be successful in their home country. Nevertheless, they adorn missionaries with halos for their lives of sacrifice, and in some cases will even sacrifice to send them back to the "heathen land." But let an articulate missionary on furlough deliver a decently organized message, to which response is good, inevitably there are those who will say, "Why don't you get a pastorate here at home? You're too good to waste your life away on the foreign field."

Being a missionary is a complicated affair. Let it be said with emphasis that the foreign mission field needs people with the best of qualifications—academically, spiritually, and also emotionally. Missionaries must be practical. Many of them are not, when they first arrive on the field, but they must have the capacity to learn to do things they would never be expected to do at home.

A high degree of ingenuity had to be evidenced by a missionary on our station the day the termite-weakened support poles of the outhouse gave way under the weight of the occupant—one of our single ladies—who plunged into the twenty-foot pit. Her rescue accomplished, the hero then turned his attention to the repair of the offending structure in order to forestall another emergency!

Even being a practical person is not enough. Missionaries are expected to be diplomats, at times moving in the circles of presidents, prime ministers, governors, and ambassadors. They must be pastors, teachers, accountants, counselors, trouble-shooters, and administrators, not to mention linguists extraordinaire. When churches consider supporting a missionary, their expectations are high. He or she must have all of the above qualifications and more.

A missionary must be able to communicate with, and relate meaningfully to, people of another culture and language. Otherwise, how could they effectively reach them with the gospel? Language study, therefore, is an area where discipline and diligence as well as intelligence are required.

The Kakwa people, for example, with their strange culture and their seemingly unintelligible language, were a challenge to us. It distressed us that so many of the Kakwa people at Adi did not understand Bangala as we had thought they would. In order to converse with them or to preach to them, it was necessary to go through an interpreter, a cumbersome procedure. We wanted to learn to communicate with them directly.

We expressed to our field director rather lavishly our love for the people and the work at Adi, and the hope that we would not be moved again. We let him know we wanted to put down roots in that country.

"You like it here, do you!" responded Mr. Van Dusen, pricking up his ears. "Well, if you want to become permanent fixtures here, learn the Kakwa language. If you get to the point where you can preach with facility in Kakwa, you will not be moved away."

Spoken like a true field director. Mr. Van Dusen really wanted us to communicate with the people, and he really meant his promise that we wouldn't be moved. The challenge of learning another language was there before us, and it didn't take us long to pick up the gauntlet. There was no Kakwa grammar, nor were Kakwa lessons available. Mr. Richardson, our predecessor at Adi and now living in South Africa, had learned the language well, but he hadn't left any materials behind. We started from scratch, therefore, using our old Bangala lessons as a guide. Pastor Yoane Akudri came in once each week to go over what we had learned. The second day of the week the head teacher came to go over the same material, and on the third day the African nurse did the same. It was a tedious but necessary process. When the three teachers didn't all agree, we had to discuss the problems with each of them a second time.

Dr. McCreery's principles from that summer at his ranch in 1938 paid off. Within a year we were both conversing with the Kakwa people in their complicated, beautifully expressive language. In another year I was preaching in it and continuing to learn to "speak with facility," as the field director had said we should. Our roots were taking hold among the people we loved. Surely we were settled in this ideal spot for a lifetime career.

One Monday morning, after preaching the day before in Kakwa with what I thought was a measure of ease and confidence, a car drove in. It was during World War II, when visiting vehicles were rare. Everyone was excited, and hundreds of black people, plus the two of us, lined the jacaranda-bordered road to welcome the car. In it were some members of the A.I.M. field council. They were in a hurry, but yes, they would stay for lunch. They had an important item of business that concerned us.

What was in the wind this time? we asked ourselves. It wasn't until after lunch, over a cup of tea, that the men disclosed what their business was.

"We've just finished our field council meeting at Aba," stated one of them with some embarrassment. His fidgeting made us suspect that something we might not like was afoot.

"We have been battling with some serious personnel problems," he continued. "Mr. Harry Stam has had a physical breakdown, and he must go home to the States. That leaves the Bible school at Aba without a director."

As the field council members continued to hem and haw, we began to get suspicious. "We've really scraped the bottom of the personnel barrel for the Stams' replacement," the speaker stammered, "and all we could come up with was you two. We have assigned you to take full charge of the Bible school and to move it from Aba to Blukwa."

Impossible. Preposterous. What about the field director's promise two years ago regarding the matter of preaching in Kakwa? What about our roots? How fickle could a field council be, assigning us to a third place in a matter of about three years? How could we move to Blukwa, where the people spoke Swahili, and neither our Bangala nor our Kakwa would be of use?

Those were disconcerting questions for the field council members, but we could see their dilemma. The Bible school program was the mission's most important ministry, or so we had always believed; and it deserved priority. The Lord was presenting us with a new challenge. Had we any right to pout about it, or to feel sorry for ourselves? Edythe shed a tear or two; but the Lord gave us the grace to be flexible and move into still another situation. We hadn't yet realized that accepting new challenges was to be the pattern of our lives.

The council members knew it was unreasonable to ask us to move a third time, but they saw no other possibility. They were relieved when we finally agreed to accept that assignment. They reassured us, prayed with us, and told us to relocate as soon as possible. Some years later, when I was assigned to the field directorship, I learned firsthand to appreciate such dilemmas.

Moving from Adi to Blukwa wasn't easy. First of all, it had to be done in haste, since the field council decision to move the Bible school away from Aba was made in September, and the new school year was to begin in January at Blukwa. Within those three months we were expected to move, get a classroom ready, and provide housing for thirty-six student families. In the meantime, we were also expected to acquaint ourselves with the curriculum and the whole program. Had we not been so naive, we would have thrown up our hands in horror and cried, "Impossible!"

What about our own housing? The council assured us that it would be no problem. A nice new guest house at Blukwa would be placed at our disposal. Also, the field council assured us, they would do everything in their power to facilitate the move and to get us started.

Mr. Amstutz came over with his army truck, since in our three years at Adi we had accumulated quite an array of household goods—most of it manufactured right in our own carpenter shop. We wondered if it would survive the long, bumpy journey. The farewell from Adi was tearful, as goodbyes always are. I find goodbyes abominable.

We arrived at Blukwa after dark, following the big truck with our own pickup. We pulled up to the guest house and were starting to unload when we were greeted by the station superintendent. To our surprise, he had not been consulted about our occupancy of the guest house. There had been a breakdown of communications somewhere between the field council and this station superintendent. Now he was understandably miffed—and adamant. The Blukwa missionaries had sacrificed to build this guest house, and they were not about to turn it over as a Bible school workers' residence.

What could we do? To go back to Adi, 250 miles away, was impossible. Where was the field council now with their promises of help? It would have been easy for us to crawl under the truck and weep.

Our good friends, Eldo and Verna Epp, who had a big old house there, took the weary pilgrims into their care. But the Epps also had a family. To share the house with them for a few days would be workable, but other arrangements would soon have to be made. Behind their home was a one-room storehouse. This was cleaned up, whitewashed, varnished, and two days later we were moved into it. It too would do for a while, but we would have to begin building a house for ourselves.

Mr. Epp then furnished us with brick, tiles, and lumber. Jim Bell, a missionary from Georgia, came from the Pygmy forest with bricklayers and a carpenter. Within one week we had a nice little three-room brick house with tile roof. Mr. Bell put in ceilings and plastered walls before leaving. Within several more weeks we had made and installed doors and windows. Then that little bungalow responded readily to Edythe's creative touch and became our home.

Bible school ministry was to be our life for the next twelve years.

NINE
BIBLE SCHOOL
MINISTRY

A hectic three months followed our arrival at Blukwa. Thirty-six African huts for student housing were built, and a carpenter shop was converted into a classroom. Tons of corn, millet, manioc, and sweet potatoes had to be bought to feed the students until their own gardens began to produce. Evenings were spent boning up on the subjects we would be teaching.

In mid-January we met our first Blukwa class, feeling overwhelmed by the importance of the job as well as by our total lack of experience. There were "extenuating circumstances," as the field council had said; in wartime new missionaries were not coming out.

Our move meant picking up yet another language, Swahili, to be learned in whatever spare time we could find beyond our Bible school commitments. The curriculum there, however, was to continue in Bangala, since it was the only Bible school for our whole field at the time. At least twelve different tribes were represented in any single class. Although one of the entrance requirements was that students should know Bangala, Swahili was to be reckoned with if we were going to communicate with the people around Blukwa. Thus, within another year we were conversing and preaching in Swahili, our third language learned during our first term of service.

Class routine at the Bible school was far from dull. When

we introduced the study of systematic theology to those students of animistic background, fellow missionaries expressed doubts. Pouring theology down the intellectual gullets of these people, who were unused to abstract concepts, would be like pouring water on a duck's back—so some people thought.

In the classroom we found the opposite to be true. Systematic theology contends first of all for the existence of God. That presented no problem. We set forth the argument of *tradition* as a proof for the authenticity of the Bible—namely, that many folklore stories in non-Christian cultures closely resemble the ancient historical accounts of the Bible. Such stories were preserved by being passed by word of mouth from one generation to the next, and they include parallels of the biblical record of the creation, fall of Adam, flood, Babel, the patriarchs, and so on. After one such lecture, a student volunteered the following:

"I know just what you mean, *bwana*. Allow me to relate a story that my father told me, which in turn had been told him by his father, and so on for many generations.

"Long ago there was an earth-chief who rebelled against the great benevolent chief of the sky. This earth-chief was tired of being submissive to his superior, so he got his many followers to plant a fast-growing tree. This tree the earth-chief dunged and watered and pruned. In years to come the tree grew far far into the heavens. The earth-chief commanded his warriors to sharpen their machetes and their war axes, and to fasten them into their cowhide belts. They were all instructed to follow him up the tree into heaven, cut a hole in the sky and enter in to fight the sky-chief and his cohorts. They were not to be fearful, for they were going to make their name the greatest in the universe. If they failed, they would be scattered through the earth, and their language would become all muddied up and would no longer be clearly understood.

"The earth-chief and his warriors began to scale the tree. Up and up they went until they thought surely they had reached heaven. They were ready to start the war.

"But all the time the earthies were climbing, the chief of the sky was watching. He knew exactly what those little rebels were up to, so he sent down the termites. Tons of them. They began to bore through the roots of the tree. All of this time the earth-men were climbing up and preparing for battle.

"At a signal given by the sky-chief, the termites put forth every effort in their attack on the roots of the tree. The giant of the forest began to tremble. There was an alarming swaying of the great limbs. Soon the branches began to convulse and to make creaking noises. Gradually the tree began to lean farther and farther, like a giant warrior wounded in battle. Then it toppled over with a thunderous crash. And what about the earthies? No, they were not killed, but they were scattered far and wide. In fact, they were strewn to the ends of the earth.

"The devastating result was that, from then on, their language was no longer understood by those scattered afar. The talk of strangers became a babble of unintelligible sounds."

The student told this story with eloquence and graceful gestures. Like his fellow students, he was a master in the art of storytelling. The whole recitation, a remarkable parallel to the Genesis account of the Tower of Babel, underscored the proposition that theologians propound as the traditional argument for the authenticity of the Bible.

The ancient ancestors of these black students had a knowledge of God and his doings that had been handed down from generation to generation. Others in the class volunteered traditions that had been passed on to them from their tribes, and they, too, corresponded with the same striking similarity to ancient Bible history.

Animistic Africans are responsive to the gospel, and it was in the Bible school that we could discover the roots of their religious beliefs. That enabled the students to hone their evangelistic techniques to a sharper edge.

Animism attributes every phenomenon to some action of the spirit world. When a woman becomes pregnant, it is because the spirit world is happy with that particular clan, and grants them increase in numbers. If a woman has a miscarriage, it is caused by angry spirits. The energy-giving sun and the life-preserving rain; the abundance of harvest, good health, successful hunts, food and water; peace with neighboring tribes, and so on, are the result of a happy and un-offended spirit world beaming upon them. Every hardship—such as a toothache, illness, death, war, drought, famine, unsuccessful hunts, etc.—is the result of an offended spirit world taking vengeance on recalcitrant people.

Animists believe in two supreme beings. One is Mungu, who is benevolent and good. The other is Jaboro, who is the scoundrel we call the devil. Mungu never takes offense and never sends any evil. Jaboro literally will raise hell with them if he is in any way offended. So, according to African reasoning, if Mungu is benevolent, why worry too much about him? Conversely, if Jaboro is malevolent, they should do whatever they can to keep him happy. That may require sacrifice, self-torture, and even death, but it is the only way the clan can survive.

It is tantamount to a modern Mafia concept. Keep the Mafia of the spirit world happy with bribes and payoffs. By way of comparison, good old Uncle Sam wouldn't hurt anyone, so why worry about cheating him on your income tax return? What does it matter if one is dishonest or disloyal with him? He's a nice guy, so don't get too excited about him. But the Mafia are another story. They won't be happy without payoffs and bribes. The supreme goal of the animist is to keep the Mafia appeased.

When Christians come with the gospel, the animist sits up and takes notice. "What was that again? What about Yesu Kristu?" A Christ who exorcised demons? Animists fear death above all else, as missionaries who have witnessed their death dances and heard their death wails well know.

Tell them about Yesu Kristu who kicked death in the teeth at Nain by raising the widow's dead son to life, and you've got a village of earnest listeners. Tell them about Jairus's daughter being raised from the dead. About Lazarus. Jesus was raised from the dead and lives forever? Animists will listen to the gospel, because they see in it a way of escaping the menacing Mafia of the real underworld.

In the classroom we discussed the approach that Christians should take in reaching animistic people. The students felt that missionaries often try to establish a European type of church organization. The order of service, type of music,

66

use of drums *vs.* use of a piano, type of marriage service, and Communion service were all matters about which the students had firm opinions. Such details, they were convinced, should be African rather than European-related. We had to agree.

In the 1970s, political leaders, headed by President Mobutu himself, and church leaders, headed by Dr. Bokeleale (president and legal representative of Eglise du Christ au Zaire), are champions of the restoration of African cultural patterns and values. Our Bible students and pastors stand with them. They believe that in matters of church polity, orders of service, and conventions of the church, they should follow African patterns and African decorum as long as they do not conflict with biblical standards.

When the war ended, more A.I.M. staff began to come out. and we were able to go home on our first furlough, weary but enthusiastic about our work. Mr. and Mrs. Ed Schuit took over from us at Blukwa, and Peter and Mary Lou Stam arrived specifically for Bible school work.

The field council in the meantime decided that there should be two general Bible schools: one in Swahili at Blukwa, and one in Bangala back at Aba. Edythe and I were then asked to establish a new pastors' school in the Bangala language designed to take graduates of the other two schools. And would you believe it, this pastors' school was to be built at Adi. We were thrilled.

When we met Peter and Mary Lou after our furlough, we discussed with them the field council's decisions about Bible schools. We both felt strongly that to have the general Bible school and the pastors' school separated would not be in the best interests of the work. By having them both at Adi we could pool our equipment and facilities as well as teaching staff. We proposed this to the field council, and they agreed that we could establish both schools at Adi.

Thus it was that we and the Stams were brought together at Adi. Peter and I were to become known as "the two Petes," and we became quite a pair—with many things in common, yet in many ways quite opposite. We were both of Dutch heritage, we both had Irish wives, we both drove Fords, we both were fond of language study, we both had rather short fuses attached to our Dutch tempers. In fact, one missionary wag conferred an "honorary P.H.D." on each of us. He called us the two Pig-Headed Dutchmen.

It didn't take the two Petes long to size up certain factors. We learned that it was better to air our feelings frankly than to hold them in. We had our fusses, but we always insisted on settling them before retiring for the night. We both had to pray much for grace "to disagree without being disagreeable and to differ without being difficult."

Our relationship with the Stams grew into a friendship that still endures. We continued to be associated with them until Edythe and I moved to Bunia in 1961. Soon after that, I was appointed to be the Zaire field director, and Peter Stam was moved to Toronto to become A.I.M.'s Canadian home director.

TEN
BIBLE
TRANSLATION

We always thought it regrettable that we never had more language study than we did. Nowadays the A.I.M. and other missionary organizations try to provide such study for all new missionaries. But in those earlier years the "extenuating circumstances" seemed to make the optimum impossible in some cases.

Our three languages—Bangala, Kakwa, and Swahili—served us well in communicating with the Africans. But we also had to deal with Belgian officials. To do so in an African language was embarrassing; they made it obvious that speaking Bangala or Swahili to another white person was very much beneath their dignity.

Belgians are bilingual, using either French or Flemish. The French I had studied in high school was very feeble. But Flemish, while spoken in quite a different dialect, was identical to the Dutch in its written form that I had been exposed to as a child in the Christian Reformed church. I therefore sent for a Dutch grammar and was soon able to converse in Flemish—not with the guttural glamor of the Flemings, but with the Netherlands accent. Because we spoke their language, we gained many lasting friends among the Flemish people in the (then) Belgian Congo.

Translation is a phase of language work that can be gratifying to missionaries. As a member of the Bangala Bible translation committee, I was asked to translate certain of the Old Testament prophetic books into Bangala. Before that time we had only the Bangala New Testament.

An African translator named Ofeni Kanda worked tirelessly for more than sixteen years on the translation of the Bible. It was a thrill to see him work, and to go over the translations with him. After the Bible was translated, Ofeni enrolled in the Bible school at Adi.

We waited many months for the Bangala Bibles to arrive from the British and Foreign Bible Society in England. One day our mail courier returned from Aba with some letters and a package. (This courier was sent to Aba by bicycle once a week, a round trip of 180 miles, and sometimes he would return with nothing—which caused us all to feel gloomy.) The package contained six advance copies of the Bangala Bible, beautifully bound, with shiny black covers and bright red edges. One Bible was especially for Ofeni, with an inscribed word of appreciation from the general secretary of the Bible Society for Ofeni's untiring work in helping to create this translation.

We took the Bible to him while the class was in session. Talk about excitement! The whole class wanted to fondle the Bible at the same time. Ofeni's reaction was unforgettable. There were tears in his eyes as he leafed through the Book, some of which fell on the bright new pages. Finally, in a voice thick with emotion he hugged the Bible to his breast and said, "Lord, let now thy servant depart in peace, for mine eyes have seen thy salvation . . . a light to the Gentiles and a glory to thy people."

The missionaries' greatest contribution to the church in Africa is to have translated the Bible into African languages. That task was not easy.

When work on the New Testament started in the twenties, Harry Stam and Mabel Gingrich worked endlessly to find just the right words. At one point they were searching for the Bangala equivalent of the verb "to write." Writing was new to these people and strange to their culture.

In order to get the word, Mr. Stam started to write on the blackboard and asked his class, "What am I doing?" The immediate response was *kunyata*. After verification by others, *kunyata* was accepted as the Bangala word for "to write," and was used in the Bible and hymnbooks, as well as in schoolbooks.

Later Mr. Stam was at the garage for a repair job on his old Chevrolet. The job entailed the removal of the cylinder head. The missionary came back as the job was nearing completion and heard the Belgian head mechanic advise his helper, *Nyati ye malamu*, as he was cinching down the head bolts. The use of a form of *kunyata* in that situation puzzled the translator, and he asked the mechanics if they were using it in the right sense. Both the Belgian and the African assured Mr. Stam that it was correct.

Confused, the translator/professor again approached his class with the problem. He began to write on the blackboard. Then, facing the class, he asked, "What am I doing?" The unanimous response was *kunyata*.

Next the khaki-clad teacher wheeled a bicycle into the classroom. Without a word he took out a wrench and proceeded to tighten the nuts on the back axle. The class was puzzled, and wondered whether their professor had gone a bit crazy. Suddenly Mr. Stam straightened up his lanky frame and asked the same question.

"*Yo azi kunyata!* (You are writing)," chorused the class.

Thoroughly confused, Mr. Stam said, "I don't understand. When I write, you call it *kunyata*. When I squeeze down the nut on the axle, you call it the same. Why do you use the same word for the two actions?"

One of the men in the class was immediately on his feet. "Why, that's very simple, *Bwana* Stam. When you *nyati* the nut on the axle, you are squeezing it down. When you *nyati* with the little white stick, you are squeezing the words right out of the end of it. What's so difficult about that?"

So it was that the word *kunyata* became the Bangala equivalent of "to write," and it was thus used for many years in the Bangala Bible. In the recent revision, however, the correct Bangala word, *kukoma*, was used.

Working with a foreign language is not without its humor. One of our Belgian official friends married a flashing and flaming Fleming. The young official was justly proud of his beautiful wife and very much in love with her. In due course, the bride became pregnant, and the husband was on cloud nine. Each time we saw him during the ensuing nine months he would give us a blow by blow account of her morning sickness and her expanding girth.

When the day of delivery finally arrived, the husband's elation gave way to *angst*. The young mother-to-be was having trouble in giving birth. After hours of agonizing effort by the mother, and miles of treading the maternity ward hallway carpet by the father, the robust baby made his appearance with a healthy wail. Papa's *angst* gave way to a state of euphoria such as he had never known.

When later we went to see them, the Belgian Papa gave a detailed description of his wife's pangs and pains. He wanted to tell the whole story in his best guttural English rather than Flemish. Edythe must hear this direct.

He made good progress in relating his tale until he was stumped for the proper obstetric term for such an abnormal delivery. His limited gynecological jargon just couldn't come up with the proper term.

Surmising the problem, Edythe suggested, "Perhaps it was a breach delivery."

"Ja, Ja, Madam!" exclaimed the father. "That is right! The baby came out britches first!"

ELEVEN
EVANGELISM

It always delights us to hear an African pastor deal with an African seeker. It's just as natural for him to talk about Christ as about his garden. Old Yakoto Ata was a master at winning his own people for Christ. One time I met him on the path and saw that he had a soiled piece of paper in his hand. Thinking he had received a letter, I asked him if he had good news from a friend.

"Ah, this?" replied Pastor Ata. "This paper contains the names of all the *paganos* in my neighboring villages. There are more than thirty of them. I use the paper every morning when I go out to the anthill in my garden to pray. The paper sharpens my thoughts so that I can remember their names and pray for them. I also make it a point to visit each one at least once every week."

Imagine that sort of consistent plan for winning his neighbors to Christ. It was not only his mind that was sharpened through the paper, but also his heart. That was clear as he stood up to pray in the public services. His face was aglow as he named his neighbors in prayer.

Several months later he showed me the slip again—the same paper, only now a bit more soiled and a bit less legible. This time at least a dozen names had *x*'s after them. "These," explained the pastor, "have now accepted Yesu Kristu. They are born again."

His evangelism technique was simple but systematic. Followed by his shenzi dog, Ata made his appearance at one of his cronies' villages. He sat on a little *kitipala* (stool) offered him by his host. Chickens scratched about, looking for an unwary worm. A frog, at which both men spat, leaped into their midst. (To miss the frog would indicate a lack of expectorating expertise.) Children sat naked on the ground, chewing on sugar cane. Inside the cookhouse a goat was bleating. The twelve-year-old boy had forgotten to stake him out in the grass, and the noisy little animal was hungry and thirsty.

The conversation was typical. They talked about the leopard that strayed into the compound the night before, jumped on a hut and broke through the thatched roof, and ran off with a newborn calf. They talked about the sick mother-in-law, and especially about the baby that had died since Ata's last visit. Ultimately, the subject of the "spirit Mafia" came up. They must be angry with his family, the host would say. Otherwise, why would his baby have died, and his mother-in-law be sick, and why the leopard invasion? He would have to call in the witch doctor to appease the spirits' anger.

Deftly Ata changed the course of the conversation. He talked about Yesu Kristu, who had power beyond that of the offended spirits.

No wonder that so many of Yakoto Ata's unsaved neighbors turned to the Lord. Ata had been praying for them every morning. Now he was there in person, cultivating the soil of the heart, planting the seed, watering it, and waiting for the miracle of the new birth.

Problems of race and culture make the job of evangelism delicate for a foreign missionary. Once an educated young African tossed a large bunch of keys into my hands. As I caught them I began to jingle them and asked him what he wanted me to do with them.

"Look at them, *monsieur*!" He was playing a game with me, and there was a mischievous gleam in his eye. "Those keys," he continued, "are what you white people have given to the blacks."

"Well, isn't that good?" I countered jokingly. "Now you have locks to protect your property. You also have a very big bunch of keys to jingle in your pocket. That will show your neighbors what a man of wealth and importance you are."

The young fellow, who was usually in blithe spirits, sobered and said, "Let me tell you a true story that took place in my village when I was a small boy.

"My father was a great hunter. Often he would go away for weeks at a time on a hunt, while the rest of the family went to my mother's village for a visit. We could leave all our property in the hut, knowing that the only prowlers we had to fear were white ants and rats. As far as *wizis* (thieves) breaking in, there was no danger.

"To lock the house, Father would simply slide a grass mat in front of the doorway and secure it with a piece of sisal string. On the mat he would tie a charm, consisting of a leopard's tooth, hairs from an elephant's tail, the wishbone of a rooster, and a chicken claw. That charm would protect our property. No one would dare to remove it, lest he invoke the wrath of the spirit world. To enter that charmed hut would be certain death.

"One day a Belgian official came to our village and saw a hut protected with such a charm. He was inquisitive about the arrangement, and my people were embarrassed to talk about it—but the irreverent white man finally elicited the whole story from the villagers. The Belgian began to laugh. He ridiculed the whole idea as ignorant superstition. 'Afraid of evil spirits, are you? Well, watch this!' With one scornful sweep of his hand he tore the charm from the doorway, threw it on the ground, and began to trample it into the dust.

"The villagers looked on in horror, expecting the barbaric Belgian to be killed instantly by the offended spirits. To the dismay of my people, nothing happened."

My young friend paused. "Mr. Brashler, with that one irreverent act, our faith in the spirit world began to shatter. Had the witch doctors been deceiving us? If the spirits did not kill this intruder, would they really kill any thief? Doubts crept in and our 'property protection' began to dissipate. Our young people began to engage in petty thieving. The charms became impotent. Today we must rely on the inadequacy of lock and key for 'property protection,' just as you white people do."

I shared that sobering narrative with my Bible school students, to whom it was no surprise. They knew that faith in the witch doctor and his charms was crumbling in the villages. This, the students declared, was good only if we could substitute something better. Far better to be governed by taboos and charms than not to be governed at all.

One of Africa's problems is that foreigners have invaded the continent and undermined the Africans' faith in the old way of life without offering a better alternative. Anthropologists contend that it is far better to leave African culture, with its taboos and superstitions, undisturbed.

Those considerations raise a crucial question. Is it better for missionaries to stay in their own countries and let Africans enjoy the false sense of security provided in their folkways? If the mission's aim is merely to introduce American or European civilization through education and philanthropy, then my answer is an emphatic "yes." But ours is the infinitely higher aim of giving Africans a true sense of security by introducing them to Christ and offering a new style of living that comes only as a result of regeneration by God's Holy Spirit.

Africans have their own authentic culture, which suits them well in many ways. There are indeed certain practices that conflict with biblical norms, such as witchcraft, polygamy, divorce, sacrifices, and so on. These must be replaced with practices that conform to biblical standards. But the Bible is supracultural, and it did not derive from the western world.

Bible school students carried a full academic load to prepare themselves for the task of presenting the gospel to their own people in an effective manner. They studied from early morning until late at night, five and one-half days per week. On Saturday afternoons and Sundays, they laid aside their books and went off for evangelism. Edythe and I were expected to do the same.

At Blukwa we had met the territorial administrator, in this case a well-educated and aristocratic Belgian. When we asked this official for permission to conduct evangelistic meetings at the Djugu prison, written permission was readily granted for a meeting each Sunday afternoon.

The next Sunday we drove into the prison compound with several students. The guards received us cordially when we showed them our document from the administrator, and ushered us into a large open courtyard where several hundred prisoners awaited us.

The prisoners were a rough-looking lot. They were chained together in groups of four or five, an iron band riveted around each neck with a length of chain four feet long connecting one prisoner to another. Filthy, covered with itch and vermin, they wore scowls that would scare the toughest of characters. As we looked out over this fearsome crowd seated on the ground before us, the prospects for a gospel meeting seemed hopeless.

We had barely begun the service when there was an interruption. A boorish and uninhibited white man burst into the courtyard and abruptly stopped the meeting. Announcing himself as the Belgian director of the prison, he threatened to lock us up unless we got out fast.

I spoke cautiously to the ruffian in Flemish, showing him the letter from the administrator—who was his superior. My use of Flemish and the letter rather softened him toward Edythe and me, but he unceremoniously ordered the African pastors out and told them never to come back. We later discovered that this director was fanatically opposed to Protestants, but he could not countermand the orders from the administrator.

He agreed to let us continue with the service, but it was to be only Edythe and I. There was to be no music. Further, we were to go to his house twice every Sunday to report our arrival and departure. We thanked him and proceeded with the service.

On ensuing Sundays we reported there, but usually found him sleeping—which meant a long wait while his wife mustered courage to awaken him. But the long waits were also in God's plan. The director's wife could speak nothing but Flemish, so she was cut off totally from social functions and literally had no friends. We found her lonely and very anxious to have a chat with us in her own language. She looked forward eagerly to our Sunday afternoon visits, and it was through her that we finally got through to her husband.

In time he thawed out completely and was actually cordial to us. He, too, began to look forward to our Sunday afternoon visits, and finally the Belgian cup of coffee was introduced. He and his wife even drove the twenty miles to Blukwa to visit us over a weekend. In time we became close friends of this man and his wife and had many occasions to explain the gospel to them. After leaving on furlough, we also corresponded with them a number of times.

Meanwhile, back at the prison, we were having our troubles. In the open courtyard the prisoners sat chained together, glaring at us. What could we say to such renegades? The gospel was indeed the "power of God to every creature," we knew, but how could we make it relevant to these men? The first service was very short, and we felt that our efforts fell flat. Hostility was everywhere.

One old character, to whom I had somehow been drawn during the service, seemed even worse than the rest. As he lingered in the courtyard, chained to three other men, I mustered up what nonchalance I could and greeted him, asking his name. His eyes were defiant as he looked me over from head to toe in disgust. Finally he grunted that his name was Gbatsi.

"Gbatsi," I said, "do you know that God loves you?"

"Loves me!" he scoffed. Then he began to laugh. "Maybe God loves you white people, but he surely does not love us prisoners. To you he has given comfortable homes and good clothing. You have your automobiles and your freedom, and good health and food on top of it. But look at us blacks. What have we got? Don't come around with such lies about God's love."

The next Sunday we were back. There was no response other than more hateful glances. But I made it a point to confront Gbatsi again.

"Salamu sana (their greeting of peace), Gbatsi, how are you? Do you know that God loves you?"

His scowl was intense. "You white man," he roared. "Get out of this prison with your lies. What do you mean, God

78

loves me? Look at these chains. Look at this filth. I live worse than an animal of the forest. Further, if God loves me, then why do I have to eat the whip on my backside? Look at this."

He turned his back to me and pulled up his shorts. His legs were lashed open and blood was trickling down his calves. He had been beaten that very morning.

Shocked, I continued. "Gbatsi, why are you in prison?"

"I murdered my wife, that is why. I have been sentenced to twenty years of this hell-hole."

"Why did you take the whip today?" I asked. To this he responded that he had broken one of the prison rules.

"Then is it not right and just that you are here? You commit murder, you are sentenced to prison. You break the prison rules, you are flogged. Those are the consequences of your disobedience."

"Oh, yes," he replied. "Now you are talking of justice, which I understand perfectly. I'm not fussing about being in prison, or about the whip. But you—you are yacking about God's love, and it's a lie."

"Gbatsi," I responded, "you understand about justice, and about laws and penalties for broken laws. My chief in heaven has the same kind of justice. If we break his laws, as we all have, then we are banished into the prison house of hell.

"Now, I have another question. When you lay down in the dust this morning to take the whip, was there anyone here who volunteered to take the lashes for you? When you were sentenced to prison, was there anyone who volunteered to serve your sentence for you?"

"*Muzungu* (white man)," Gbatsi said, "I don't understand you. Of course there were no volunteers to substitute for me. I murder and it is I, Gbatsi, who goes to prison. I disobey and it is I, Gbatsi, who takes the whip. What is this nonsense about a substitute?"

I opened my Bible to Isaiah 53:5. "But he was wounded for our transgressions, he was bruised for our iniquities: the chastisement of our peace was upon him; and with his stripes we are healed." Then I read 1 Peter 2:24. "Who his own self bare our sins in his own body on the tree . . ."

Gbatsi became pensive. Finally he said, "*Muzungu*, if you

are lying to me, I warn you. Don't come back to this prison, because I will kill you. But if what you say is true, I want to know the whole story."

The next Sunday we returned with the same message, a message of love but also of justice. Gbatsi, still chained to his partners in crime, was there—but not with his former hostility. He was anxious to hear and learn.

Some weeks later he accepted the Savior, and his heart overflowed with joy in his complete transformation. He was illiterate, so a Bible did him no good. After that, he usually held the hymnbook upside down when he sang, but he soon knew the words perfectly. His memory was phenomenal. Every Sunday afternoon he memorized several Scripture passages and retained them. He also learned to pray.

The prisoners' beds consisted of nothing more than sixteen-inch planks suspended between pairs of brick balustrades, just far enough apart for the neck chains to reach from plank to plank. Every night Gbatsi gathered some of the chain gangs together in his ward to study the verses, to discuss the last Sunday's sermon, and to pray.

One Sunday I saw a new face. This man seemed very receptive. After the meeting I made my way to him and asked what he thought of the message. He beamed as he said, "Oh, *bwana*, those are very good words. Gbatsi explained them all to me as I lay on my plank. I have finished planting them in my heart, and I am now a believer in Christ."

Amazing grace. Gbatsi the killer was now a soul-winner. A month or so later I noticed that he had lost his neckpiece. The rivets had been cut, and the iron band had been taken from his neck. There were calluses and scar tissue where it had bitten into his neck for many years.

That Sunday I again confronted the prison director. He seemed unusually friendly, but he asked rather abruptly, "What have you done to Gbatsi?"

I feared another unpleasant scene with him, so I answered defensively. "I have done nothing to Gbatsi except preach the gospel to him. Is there something wrong?"

The director smiled. "I don't know what you mean by preaching the gospel, but whatever that is, it has completely changed his life. For years he has been ringleader of the troublemakers. Whenever there was a riot, or any kind of trouble, Gbatsi was at the center of it. He has been whipped more than any other prisoner in the whole block. Since this gospel has got hold of him, he has changed into a model prisoner. Did you notice that I removed his neck band? Now he is one of my *kapitas* (trustees), with a gang of men under him, working on the road. This gospel must really be something. Keep on coming with it."

It was still wartime, and gas was becoming as scarce as luxuries in the prison. Making the twenty-mile trip from Blukwa to the prison each Sunday was becoming more and more difficult. I mentioned this to the director, expressing doubts as to whether I'd be able to come the following week.

The Belgian brushed off my objection. "You will be here," he said. "*Mungu* (God) will see to that." His faith was greater than mine, I thought. But the director had something else in mind.

One morning several days later, we heard a commotion at the front door. There were two prisoners with a soldier, the latter with a whip in his hand. All three of them greeted me warmly, for were they not of my parish? The two prisoners shouldered a sapling pole, about eight feet long, between them. Dangling from the pole was a forty-liter gas drum, tied to it with strips of bark. The men were sweating and panting as they dropped their burden on our front veranda. Their shoulders were sore and bleeding where the pole's weight had cut into their flesh.

The soldier explained. "The director of the prison sent us here this morning with forty liters of gas. He said you must use it to come to the prison on Sunday, because he wants you to preach the gospel to the prisoners. Oh, yes—he wants you to bring the empty container back next Sunday, so he can send you more."

The Belgian official had been right. *Mungu* did see to it, as he had said the Sunday before. He did not tell us that he was going to enter into a conspiracy with *Mungu* in order to see this miracle performed, but no doubt he had been working on the plan when we last saw him. Our hearts were warmed at the response of that Belgian official, and in particular at the ungrudging attitude of the two prisoners. This was more than ten gallons of gas, carried over the sharp gravel road for all of twenty miles. Without a doubt, the gospel had made its impact on that Belgian's hard heart.

As for Gbatsi, he served out his twenty years; but those last years after his conversion were in many ways happy ones. Since then he has died and met the One who became his substitute lash-taker.

TWELVE
THE NATIONAL CHURCH IN MISSION

According to missiologists, the indigenous church should rest firmly on a tripod of three "separate selves": self-government, self-support, and self-propagation. That tripod is basically sound, and it reflects a goal we work toward on the mission field. A good example of self-propagation is found in the Adi church's evangelizing the Pygmies.

James Bell was the "southern gentleman" missionary who helped us put up the brick house at Blukwa. His wife Agnes was the daughter of Charles Hurlbert, general director of the A.I.M. for twenty years during its pioneer period. Edythe and I took a special liking to Jim and Agnes Bell and adopted them as second parents. While we were still at Adi, we invited them to visit us. This was no new territory to the Bells. They were the ones who had begun and established the work among the Lugbara and the Kakwas. Later they opened up Oicha, down in the Pygmy forest.

Jim was never happy as our guest unless he had something to do. So we asked him if he would preach to the Adi church, telling them how the work among the Pygmies was begun. He was more than ready to accede to the request, and the meeting was set for the following afternoon.

The church was packed with people at the appointed time. Many of the old-timers remembered the Bells from twenty years earlier and were thrilled to welcome them back. The prolific results of planting the gospel seeds were obvious in the large crowd that now gathered in the church, a gratifying sight to the Bells.

Pastor Yoane Akudri led the meeting, and his heart melted as he presented his old *Tata* (Father) Bell. Jim, too, was a soft-hearted man, and his sermon was punctuated with tears —tears of joy because of the achievement among the Kakwas and tears of sadness because of the paucity of preachers to enter the wide-open door into the Pygmy forest.

In his sermon he told how they had left Adi to establish an outpost at Oicha, and how Dr. and Mrs. Carl Becker followed them to begin a hospital work in the forsaken forest.

After moving into their mud-hut home, the Bells spent their evenings in the clearings under the magnificent moon that shimmered through the giant trees. They listened to the music of the primeval forest: the bawling of the African bush babies, the hooting of owls, the beeping of hideous fruit bats, the laughing of hyenas, the barking of wild dogs. These sounds blended into a symphonic poem reminding them that God their Father was the creator of this setting, the composer of this medley.

But there was a dissonant note. From the heart of the giant forest came the silent cry of hundreds of thousands of small forest people, estranged from their Maker. The thought of this not only drove the melody out of the music; it also drove sleep from their weary bodies. How to reach these mini-mortals was the thought that plagued them as they tossed restlessly in their camp beds.

The audience sat spellbound as Jim continued his narrative. He told of the dedicated African Christians who had gone with them to open up the forest. A road had already been cut through the jungle from Irumu to Beni, going right past Oicha. A second road had been cut from Irumu to Mambasa, toward Kisangani (then Stanleyville). Those two roads formed two sides of an almost equilateral triangle. The third imaginary side cut right through the forest, approximately one hundred miles to Mambasa. The compass indicated the direction, but this forest was totally unexplored and uncharted.

A dream then began to disturb Jim Bell's sleep. He would be God's man to conquer this "giant." He would spiritually claim God's promise to Joshua, "Every place that the sole of your foot shall tread upon, that have I given unto you ..." (Josh. 1:3).

Jim shared his dream and new determination with Agnes. Her response was this: "Jim, if you attempt this conquest, it is likely that you will die in the forest. I love you so much. What would I do without you? But, if God has laid this burden on your heart, who am I to stop you? You must go if you feel that this is his plan. I will be waiting for news of your success at this end, and I will go with you in my prayers each step of the way."

Such was the quality of the old pioneers. Jim had married a "winner." At that point in his message, it was difficult for him to go on.

He told how the Belgian authorities were not so ready to cooperate. They had the same misgivings that Agnes had, but they were adamant. Under no circumstance was he to go on this foolhardy adventure. Nevertheless, Jim had his mandate from a higher authority. God said "Go!" and Jim made his preparations. He would not be stopped by Belgian officials.

Their safari outfits were laid out. Jim had a half-dozen pairs of khaki shorts and shirts, a camp bed and bedding, a mosquito net, and a minimum of cooking gear. Food was the big item.

The outfit had been divided into a dozen porter loads, weighing approximately thirty pounds each, and at least a dozen porters were enlisted at Oicha to carry them. Three or four Lugbara Christians also became part of the team. Together they formed a motley, nondescript caravan as they began slugging their way through the forest, following the compass to a degree slightly north of west.

The going was rough, and the sharp underbrush lashed at their brawny legs. The forest was intensely hot. During the first day of battling brush and insects, they encountered not one Pygmy. They did, however, run into some chimpanzees. These creatures resented the human invasion, shrieking out their protests in a barrage of abuse.

They made camp early that first night—footsore, hungry, weary, and disappointed. Why hadn't they seen any Pygmies? After a supper of beans and coffee, they read Psalm 121. "I will lift up mine eyes unto the hills" (here Mr. Bell interpolated the word "tree-tops"), "from whence cometh my help. My help cometh from the Lord . . . he that keepeth thee will not slumber. . . . The Lord is thy keeper. . . . The Lord shall preserve thee. . . . The Lord shall preserve thy going out and thy coming in from this time forth, and even for evermore."

This was a good psalm for them; they would adopt it as their safari psalm. They would memorize it and repeat it as they marched through the forest.

The second day was ushered in by a typical tropical forest deluge that drenched them to the skin. But their spirits were only temporarily dampened. This was a new day and surely they would meet some of the Pygmies. They asked God specifically for that before they started their second day's trek.

Jim was silent as they started out. He was thinking of Agnes and of how he had fallen in love with her while sailing through the romantic South Atlantic toward the Cape. Her dad had also been on board at the time, and he seemed dignified and forbidding. Agnes was her father's favorite, and no young upstart from Georgia was going to intrude. Any man who wanted to marry the apple of the director's eye would have to meet high standards.

At times as they slugged through the miles of forest, Jim's face lit up in a smile, remembering how the Daddy Director had caught them on deck in an embrace. Again he smiled, recalling how embarrassed he had been when he finally mustered up enough courage to ask the old man for his daughter's hand. Words would not come. What a dummy he was! When he finally found his voice, the words tumbled out incoherently.

Now he grew sad. His wife was back at Oicha; when would he see her again? But he roused himself. When was he going to see the Pygmies? That was still the question at hand as they tramped through the forest. Where were those elusive little people that he had heard so much about? Jim was obsessed with the thought that the Pygmies were totally unaware of their need for Christ. That was still the burden of his message as he spoke now to the Adi church.

"Oh, Lord, where are the Pygmies?" Jim prayed as he trekked. His question was not to be answered until the seventh day of their safari. By that time everyone was exhausted and exasperated. They had decided that if they saw no Pygmies that day, they would do an about-face and head back to Oicha.

Mile after mile they trudged, waging a running battle with the cutting brush and the stinging insects. They were about ready to quit when they heard the sound of a snapping twig. They turned abruptly. There, some thirty yards from them, was a Pygmy.

They held their breath. Would he run like a hunted fawn? Would he riddle the caravan with his poisoned arrows? The missionary prayed silently and hastily.

The Pygmy stood his ground, although quivering with fright. Had he been facing a leopard or an elephant, or even a wounded buffalo, he would have known how to cope with the situation. But this, his first glimpse of a white giant, along with all these black giants, left him completely unnerved. He glanced frantically at the dense forest. Should he dart away? But no, he faced these strange men from another world as they moved gently toward him.

Mr. Bell smiled and uttered the Swahili greeting, "Salamu sana." No response. How could the man possibly understand Swahili? But a smile is universally understood, and Jim's brilliant smile with its flashing gold tooth put the Pygmy at ease. Further attempts at verbal communication were pointless. The little man made a majestic gesture toward the thick forest, indicating that the strangers were to follow him.

Follow they did, about a half mile off-course, when all at once they were in a Pygmy camp. A cluster of twig huts, about four feet high, were scattered over the clearing. Pygmy men, women, and children were all over the place, shouting excitedly. Jim later learned that although the missionary caravan had spotted no Pygmies, the Pygmies had seen the caravan the very first day. A band of scouts was always within several hundred yards of them, spying on their every move. Now they had led the intruders into their camp. But why?

A leader stepped up to Mr. Bell and muttered something unintelligible. Then he beckoned to Jim to follow him to one of the huts and motioned for him to enter. On his knees the southern gentleman wriggled into the hut, like a mongoose wriggling into its nest.

The missionary crouched down inside. When his eyes became accustomed to the darkness he saw a very small Pygmy lying on a piece of bark cloth. The man was wizened and wrinkled, and near death. Jim surmised that he had been ushered into the hut in order to perform a miracle of healing. Evidently the Pygmies had heard about the white giants out in the open country and about their ability to exorcise the evil spirits that caused sickness.

Jim was in a dilemma. To heal the man would be to gain entrance into the hearts of the people. To fail to do so would not only mean loss of face, but it might also incite a massacre of the missionary and his caravan. He had a few aspirin and some of the common remedies for ordinary sicknesses. But what were they in the face of this? Prayer was his only recourse—and pray he did, crouching on his knees on the mud floor. As he prayed earnestly in Swahili, Pygmies peered into the hut, expecting a miracle. Nothing happened.

Jim bent over the sick man, grasping his hand and speaking loudly into his ear the precious name of Yesu Kristu. Three times he uttered this name which alone could save the Pygmy. At last Jim came out of the hut, leaving the man to die. He sat down in the clearing and wept bitter tears.

Jim was again in tears as he continued his message in the Adi church. "My dear brothers and sisters, I'm not sure that I'll see that dying Pygmy in heaven. That thought chases the sleep away from my pillow at night. But one thing I do know: I did my very best for that dying man."

The congregation was in tears, too. They knew exactly what Jim was preaching about. He had first come to them in circumstances quite similar to those of his entrance among the forest people.

Jim concluded his story by telling the audience that the Pygmies were his friends from that time on. In Jim's prayer, and in his tears, they had seen real love. They then accompanied the caravan all the way to the Mambasa road, bringing fruit and nuts and killing monkeys with their arrows so that the giants could have protein.

Forty days after kissing Agnes goodbye, Jim came stumbling back to the Oicha station. He had taken a truck from Mambasa, and he hardly looked like the same man who had started the journey. His clothes were in shreds, tied to his body with strips of bark string. His last pair of canvas shoes had large holes in them, and blistered toes peeked through. His legs were ulcerous. He was skinny. Malaria had taken its toll. But Jim came back leading a band of laughing Pygmies. Trust had been established. Friends had been made. The forest people had begun to hear about Yesu Kristu.

Finally Jim looked out over the Kakwa audience (no one minded that he had preached almost two hours). "My dear Kakwa brothers and sisters, I am now an old man. There are still myriads of Pygmies to reach for Christ. You have the gospel, and your church is strong. Will you continue this outreach by giving your sons and daughters to help me finish the job?"

Jim sat down while Pastor Yoane got up to close the service. "Bandeko (brothers and sisters)," he said quietly, "this man introduced us to Christ. Now he is in the forest, doing the same for the Pygmies. It is our responsibility to help him. Let us pray."

When the meeting was over, we all went home in a subdued manner. God had spoken, and Edythe and I—along with the vast assembly—had been touched by his Holy Spirit.

The Bells returned to Oicha, but they had planted fertile seeds in the hearts of the Adi believers. Two weeks later, two fine young pastors "rang our doorbell" (the ringing of the bell consisted of raucous, persistent coughing). We opened the door to find Yonatana Wai and Yisaya Buki. "Can we talk to both of you?" they asked.

Seated on cowhide chairs on the veranda, they talked about goats, chickens, unproductive cows, crops, and sick babies. Finally they came to the point. "Bwana," declared Yisaya, "God is calling Yonatana and me to go to Oicha to help Bwana Bell evangelize the Pygmies."

What a startling answer to prayer. It was precisely these two dear pastors that Edythe and I had prayed about. They seemed such a stable pair, and so sincere. Now here they were—entirely unaware that we had talked about them, but ready to go. God was working. Or was he?

What if these two families should go the 350 miles into the forest and then become homesick? What about their diets, which would be so different? What if the forest viruses should strike them? Now that God had heard and answered our prayers, we had doubts. We expressed these doubts to the two men.

"What if sickness strikes you there, far away from your relatives? What about the strange food? You will not have granaries there stuffed with millet and manioc and corn. You won't be able to come home when the going gets tough."

Yisaya was bouncing from one foot to another. His impatience was beginning to surface. *"Bwana,"* he said, "let me ask you a question. When Yesu Kristu left his village to come to earth, did he stop to ask questions about food or housing or medical facilities? He did not! He slept on the Mount of Olives. He ate with sinners. Later the Great Apostle wrote in a letter 'Let this mind be in you that was in Christ.' Yonatana and I have prayed much, and we feel that we must go."

What can one say against such reasoning? But we were still cautious. "Have you prayed about this with your wives?" we asked. "Are they willing to go along? If God calls a husband, he also calls the wife."

Those were senseless questions, they thought. Why shouldn't their wives be willing? Wives had no choice but to obey their husbands. But we were insistent. After prayer and counseling, we told them to go home and pray with their wives. They and their wives were to come back in a week's time to meet with us and the elders of the church, so that we could see how God was leading them.

In a week all the elders were seated on our veranda. Pastor Yoane sat at a little table to chair the meeting. Finally Yisaya and Yonatana came in, followed by their wives, Sipula and Deborah. They were beautiful women, each with a baby strapped to her back. The two men each took a chair, and two more were offered to the women. They, however, ignored the chairs and sat down gracefully on the mud floor. They would not be so presumptuous as to put themselves on a level with their husbands.

Each of the two men and their wives gave a ringing testimony of God's call to them. All four were equally positive. They were ready to go and die if that was God's plan. Woe would be unto them if they did not go to preach the gospel to the Pygmies.

By now we were all convinced that this was God's will. We must get them to the Bells as soon as possible. The matter of salary was still a question, but the elders saw no problem here. These four were members of the Adi church, and the church would send them whatever salary Mr. Bell thought they should have. As it turned out, the church was faithful to that commitment for many years to come.

Within two weeks they were ready to go, and there was another packed service at the church to bid farewell to these missionaries.

By the time our old Ford pickup was loaded (two bicycles, beds, mattresses, chairs, tables, food, chickens, and children), the surrounding acre of lawn was crowded with people who had come to pray and sing the missionaries on their way. But wait, where was Deborah? All the others were packed in, ready to go—but no Deborah. Someone had seen her in her father's village about a mile away, and there had been a *shauri kubwa* (big affair). Her father was putting up a fuss. He would not let his daughter go off to die in the Pygmy forest.

Some of us walked over to the village. Deborah was in tears. Hadn't God called her to go with her husband? Hadn't her husband paid all of the cows and goats to complete her dowry? What right had her father to hold her back?

Although we tried to reason with him, he was not to be assuaged. Finally we had to take her by the hand and lead her away. The father gesticulated threateningly. "If you take my daughter to the forest, she will die. And when she dies, you will hear from me again."

But God was in this, and there seemed no other choice but to take his daughter against his wishes. We did not like to do that.

Never did a missionary have such a send-off, nor such a trip to the mission field. The three-day trip was great, with no more than the usual number of flat tires, fuel pump fusses, etc. We arrived in front of the Bells' house at Oicha in a chorus of joy.

The Bells had no way of knowing in advance that we were coming. (This was before the time of inter-station radio communication, and the telegraph and postal systems took weeks to communicate a message.) But they were thrilled by our arrival. Pastor Kasali, the Oicha pastor, was immediately summoned, and the church began to make arrangements for the newcomers. Dr. and Mrs. Becker came to greet them and to help get the families situated.

They were to be at Oicha only long enough to get what was necessary for their new homes in the forest. These "apostles to the Pygmies" began immediately to study the new language, and within a few weeks they were preaching to the forest people.

Hardships were innumerable. Both families lost children and buried them in the forest. Diets were difficult. They tried to plant gardens as they had at Adi, only to have the fruits of their labors stolen just before the crops were ready for harvest. But they were in God's place for them. Self-propagation was underway.

In the meantime we moved to Blukwa. One morning as we were teaching our classes, a car drove up. We recognized it as Jim Bell's car, and he had Pastor Yonatana with him. It was great to see them, but it was obvious that something was wrong. Yonatana said, "Bwana, Deborah was giving birth to our sixth baby out in the forest. I had wanted to take her to the maternity ward at Oicha, but she refused. She said there was too much work to be done, that we could not afford the time. God would help her. But the other day she was in labor for many hours with no one to help. At sundown she died with her unborn baby. They are buried in the forest."

What shocking news! To think that this young father was now bereft of his wife.

Then he continued his narrative. "You remember the threats of her father when we took her against his will. Now I must face him. Will you go with me to tell him?"

We left the same afternoon and arrived at Adi late at night.

Pastor Yoane was stunned by the news, as were the others. "But *bwana*," one of them said, "isn't the whole sad affair *shauri la Mungu* (the affair of God)? He cannot make a mistake. We will sleep the rest of the night and pray for God's help as we go to see Deborah's father in the morning."

The old father was sitting on his *kitipala* (stool) the next morning when he saw us. He jumped up from the stool immediately. "*Bwana* Bell, *Bwana* Brashler, my son-in-law, welcome to my poor village. It is so good to see you. Now tell me how things are with my little girl whom you whisked away to the forest." This latter remark was make jokingly and with a twinkle in his eye. At least he was friendly.

"*Ndoe na ngai* (my dear friend)," we began, "we have come with very sad news. God has seen fit to call your dear daughter up to his village in heaven." Then we proceeded to fill in every detail of the sorrowful story.

The old man sat stoically and heard us without interruption. After the story was told he sat in silence for a very long time. How should we deal with his onslaught of verbal abuse? Would he resort to violence? Neither came. At last he looked up to meet our eyes. His face was calm. There was no hostility, no sign of an outburst. Then he began to speak.

"My little girl has moved to her new hut in God's village. This makes me sad, and will cause my tears to spill over. But I know that God does not make a mistake. Mingled with my sadness, I sense gladness. I am an old man and am becoming feeble. Very soon I shall follow Deborah, and I shall have a new hut right beside hers. Since last I saw you, *bwana*, I, too, have come to believe in God's Son, Yesu Kristu. I no longer fear death and the bad spirits, for I am now a Christian."

Our joy could not be contained, and our tears began to overflow. This was the father whom we had prayed so much about and had feared so much. God had worked in his heart. Our tears were followed by shouting and joy unspeakable. We would all see Deborah again. This ex-pagan father was now our brother.

Our two Kakwa missionary families worked in the forest with the Bells, Dr. Becker, and another American A.I.M. missionary, Margaret Clapper, for more than twenty-five years. There is a growing church in the forest area, with many local congregations. One of the Pygmies recently graduated from the Bible school and is now an ordained pastor.

Yonatana and Yisaya are retired, as are Dr. and Mrs. Becker. Jim and Agnes Bell have been in heaven for almost a decade, singing the song of the Redeemer with many redeemed Pygmies. Margaret Clapper is still with the Pygmies, doing whatever she can to help them. Praise be to God.

THIRTEEN
FURLOUGH
FUROR

*Grandpa looked sternly over his spectacles down at Johnnie.
The pious patriarch had ambitions that his grandson would
someday be a missionary. At the moment, however, Johnnie
was more inclined to be a twerp.*

*"Johnnie," demanded the grandfather, "what career do
you plan to follow?"*

*"Well, Gramps," was the response, "I think I'll be a mis-
sionary on furlough."*

Furloughs are fun at times, but they are not the ideal life.
You wouldn't want a steady diet of them. There are those
who think that missionaries who look forward to their furlough have never quite attained the degree of spirituality that
their image demands. By contrast, there are some brand-new
missionaries who begin making inquiries about their trip
home almost before they clear customs on the way to their
field. Between those two opposites one can strike a happy
medium.

Furloughs are necessary and nice. We are presently on our
sixth one, and we have enjoyed each of them. Except for our
first time out, when Edythe was seriously sick in Nairobi on
our way to Congo, we have eagerly looked forward to getting
to the field and digging into a new term of service. But we
have also anticipated each furlough with the same eagerness.

We have never felt that furloughs are unspiritual and have never apologized for being on one. We believe that they are in God's plan, whether for a pastor, a Christian worker at home, or a missionary overseas. Jesus said, "Come apart and rest." (Someone enlarged on this divine injunction and said, "Come apart and rest, or you will come apart for the rest of your life.")

Our first term was a long one, six and one-half years. We were often weary and often suffered from one tropical disease or another. In spite of that, the term did not drag. We had anticipated going home after five years, but were told to "forget it." Because it was wartime, overseas travel was out of the question. Our work was meaningful and, amazingly to us at least, the months whizzed by. God's grace was always sufficient.

Furlough appeared on the horizon soon enough. Our furnishings and household effects had to be stored in an old storehouse at Blukwa, and our clothes (new for our wedding) had to be gotten out of mothballs. They looked terrible, but we tried to resurrect them with a charcoal iron and a steam cloth.

My black double-breasted wedding suit, which had been so much in style and had looked so nice at the wedding, was still in good condition except for a bit of mildew. After pressing, it looked a bit shinier than it should have, but at least it still fit. Edythe's dresses also responded well to the charcoal iron and still fit her. Neither of us had gotten fat. So our wardrobe looked adequate. My suit would last through our furlough. Someone had suggested I buy a homburg hat for our wedding. They never go out of style, I was told. Just the thing for a missionary.

Luggage was another matter. We had bought a big metal suitcase, almost as big as a steamer trunk, which had been stored for three years on the damp mud floor at Blukwa. Now, the bottom had rusted through, and it looked like a honeycomb. To get a new one was impossible. What were we to do?

Someone had said that missionaries were to be ingenious. We would have to think of some way to repair the bottom of that suitcase. The only idea that came to mind was to cut open a five-gallon kerosene can and with a pair of tin snips trim it to fit the suitcase. We then bolted this tin sheet in place and with shiny black enamel (the only kind available) painted it a brilliant hearse-black. The latch had rusted out, too, but we found that a nice piece of African sisal rope, tied neatly around the case, kept it shut. The luggage didn't look bad to us, and we were all set.

The departure date arrived, and again it was heart-rending to say goodbye to our African and missionary friends. Once we got into Uganda, traveling toward the east coast, we realized how fatigued we were. But the excitement of going shot extra adrenaline into our blood. How nice it would be to get back.

During our last year on the field, Dad had suffered a massive coronary thrombosis, and for months his life hung by the proverbial thread. We had been wondering if we would ever see him again this side of Glory. Also, Edythe's dad had undergone major surgery. It was good to be on our way toward them.

Postwar sea traffic was still congested, but God opened up a two-berth cabin for us on the sparkling new *African Star*, sailing from Mombasa, Kenya, southward through the balmy waters of the Indian Ocean. It was a cargo ship with limited accommodations for passengers.

The crew members were congenial, keen to hear about the Congo. We regaled them and the other passengers with stories about our first-term experiences. In turn, they reintroduced us to American goodies. There were apples, boxes of them (we had eaten apples only once or twice since coming to Africa). There were chocolate bars, jellybeans, dry cereal, and ice cream. We had long since forgotten how good those things were.

The three-week trip from Mombasa to New York, via the Cape of Good Hope, was wonderful. We ate, slept, played games, read, and enjoyed the ship's company. We actually gained some weight, which we both needed. Each of the three Sundays the captain asked me to conduct worship services for both crew and passengers.

Arrival in New York, with the customs and immigration procedures, came all too soon. A customs man stared at the black suitcase with the African cord tied around its middle. Then he surveyed us from head to toe, and his eye lingered for awhile on my homburg. He scrutinized my black form-fitting double-breasted suit. He didn't say anything, but just stood there and gaped. We waited, feeling awkward. What was wrong with this character?

Finally he found his voice and managed to ask, "Who are you, and where have you been?"—emphasizing the who and the where. We told him, and I started to undo the Congolese cord around the suitcase.

"Missionaries!" he blurted. "From Congo?" Suddenly his vocal cords were unleashed, and he poured forth a flurry of irrelevant questions. "How long have you been there? What did you eat? Did you have malaria? Did you see any leopards? Didn't the cannibals eat you? Have you got a monkey in that?"

By that time I had the rope untied, and the suitcase open. Clothes as well as shaving gear and assorted other paraphernalia burst out over the top. We asked him if he didn't want to examine our baggage, but he ignored the question and proceeded to ask more of his own. About this time we started to feel like freaks. Then he waved us on through. It would have been unnecessary to untie the ropes.

Outside the customs building we hailed a taxi. Our suitcase was dumped into the trunk of the cab along with the rest of our baggage. By the time we were sitting in the back seat of this Brooklyn cab, my homburg was askew, and my black polka-dot wedding necktie was in disarray. The cabby looked us over as he asked us our destination. Finally, in his Brooklyn accent, he asked, "Buddy, where did you get that hat?"

"What's wrong with this hat?" I asked with a slight touch of belligerence. "Can't you see that this is a homburg? They never go out of style."

The cabby continued his scrutiny through the rear-view mirror as he drove with reckless skill through the heavy traffic. We had never seen such traffic, certainly not for the past six and one-half years. In our part of Congo one could go for many days without seeing a moving vehicle. This was a little jarring. Edythe and I gripped each other's hands as our driver squeezed through the maze of cars.

The cabby, keeping one eye on his driving and the other on the mirror, didn't know quite how to figure us out. He had carried politicians and preachers, tycoons and toughs, moguls and movie actors, but somehow he couldn't fit us into any of those slots. Finally came the inevitable query, "Who are you and where have you been?"

Our answer elicited a whistle and a "wow." The usual flurry of questions followed. Finally he had us at our mission headquarters in Brooklyn. He let us off with minimum fare and declined our tip, giving his parting advice: "Buddy, you better get a new hat!"

I dismissed that advice, still convinced that my homburg was OK and that my suit wasn't all that bad—though I was beginning to have doubts about the latter. When we got into the mission headquarters I noticed that the men were wearing odd-shaped suits. The jackets were considerably longer, with a much fuller cut—not at all like the fancy, fit-the-curves cut of mine. Oh well, these fellows here were stuck behind desks. They couldn't possibly know the styles.

Edythe's dresses were a bit longer than those of the secretaries in the office, but Edythe was not the oddball. These Brooklyn women didn't know how funny they looked. Edythe looked great.

At last our business was done in New York City, and we were on the train, starting our long ride to the West Coast. The trip was interesting for the first several days, but the last two were boring. Why so many stops? Why such a snail's pace? Why couldn't those iron chargers up front keep up a steady ninety miles per hour? How anxious we were to arrive in Seattle.

We were finally starting to realize how long it had been since we had last seen our families. Would we look strange to them? Would they, too, be wearing strangely cut clothes? Would they look older? Excitement kept mounting by the mile, especially as we started the ascent through the Cascades. Finally, at long last, we were pulling into the Seattle station.

The train ground to a halt and we found ourselves on the platform, completely surrounded by relatives. Most of the McKees were there, and my whole family, as well as lots of others, all anxious to get a close-up and to give us a hug. We noticed lots of children whom we didn't know. They had been babies when we left, and now they were sophisticated first, second, and third graders. It would take us awhile to get to know them all.

And there was Dad! He hadn't been sure he could make the trip to Seattle to meet the train, but there he was. That he had been near to death was still very obvious. His complexion had an unnatural pallor, and his eyes were sunken. He didn't at all resemble the handsome man of six years ago. But, thank God, he was here.

Once again the outlandish baggage occupied everyone's attention. It was beginning to dawn on us that there might, after all, be something strange about our appearance. We were feeling a bit embarrassed; after all, this time it wasn't a Brooklyn cabby, but our own people who were staring at us. Too bad I couldn't have found another color paint for the suitcase instead of that shiny black.

The baggage was loaded into several cars, and Edythe got into the car with her parents—who both looked great. You can imagine the chatter on their way home. Everyone was talking at the same time, with no one bothering to finish a sentence or even to wait for an answer to the questions they asked. They had six and one-half years to catch up on in the next few hours.

I went home with my older brother and my parents. While driving through Seattle, my brother mentioned that he had an errand to do in one of the stores. Wouldn't I like to go along with him? he asked.

As he led me into the department store, he asked the same question the Brooklyn cabby had about my hat. He told me that hats were no longer in style; it would be much better to go bareheaded. But the suit bothered him even more than the hat. I tried to defend it, but he would hear none of it. It belonged to another era. He wasn't satisfied until I was fitted with a modern suit and shod with proper shoes.

Our car buzzed with talk, too, between Seattle and Everett. Why did Edythe and I both have such jaundiced complexions? Did we have yellow fever? I explained that the yellow color was due to the Atebrin we had been taking as a prophylaxis for malaria. During the war the U.S. Government had developed this treatment for G.I.s who suffered from that disease. It was far more effective, and less drastic, than the old quinine.

During our first two furloughs we were able to live in an apartment in Dad's apartment house. That was a great financial help, since it would take lots of money to outfit us for another five-year term on the field.

A mission such as the Africa Inland Mission is a sending organization with expertise in matters such as travel, obtaining necessary legal documents, forwarding money and freight shipments, and operating an effective work on the field. However, it does not have a large constituency to enable it to pay missionaries' salaries, or to finance their travel. For this the missionaries must trust the Lord, and also get out on the deputation trail to raise their own support. Philippians 4:19 has never failed us.

The mission also expects the missionary to enter into a program of self-improvement. Thus we enrolled at Everett Community College for intensive study in French. As many other courses as we could handle to help us in our Bible school ministry—sociology, anthropology, ancient and medieval history, and psychology—were pursued later at the University of Washington. Edythe also took a number of courses in music, since she taught that subject.

Each of our furloughs has been quite different. By the time we were home on our second one, we had been married for thirteen years, but had no children—a great disappointment. We had made the rounds of all our mission doctors (and also our own doctor in Everett, Dr. Westover) for tests, but none of them came up with any reason for our childless marriage. They all pronounced us healthy and told us to go home and keep trying. Try we did, but to no avail.

After arriving home on our second furlough, we stopped in Chicago. There was a Christian adoption agency there, and it seemed that God was leading us in this direction. The kind old gentleman in charge of the agency advised us to forget the idea. To adopt a baby there we would have to spend a year in

Illinois to establish residency in that state. There was a long waiting list, and further, the courts would be very reluctant to grant a baby to missionary parents going back to Africa.

That was disappointing, but we accepted it as God's will. We proceeded on to the West Coast, fully reconciled to the idea that a "fruitful vine" was not to be in our home, and that our table was not to be surrounded by "olive plants" (Ps. 128).

During our first days back, we were invited to a dinner at the home of our friends, the Westmorelands. Present at the dinner were Dr. and Mrs. Westover. They had adopted three girls, and the experience had been wonderful. Now they wanted a fourth baby, a boy.

During the course of the dinner, the doctor was called to the hospital for one of his maternity cases. A young couple had already had four babies, one right after another, and now the husband was out of work. They wanted to discuss their problem with Dr. Westover, as they thought it might be best to put up this fifth child, a boy, for adoption.

The Westovers had decided that the next available boy was to be theirs. By the time the doctor had interviewed the young couple, and the decision was firmed up that this new child was to be adopted, the dinner party was over, and Mrs. Westover was at home awaiting her husband.

"Clara," he exclaimed as he burst into the bedroom, "there's a baby boy at General Hospital available for adoption. Let's start the proceedings first thing in the morning."

"Oh, Howard," responded the wife, "I've been doing a lot of thinking these last few hours. Pete and Edythe were disappointed in not being able to adopt a child in Chicago. They would love to have one, and this may be their only chance. Let's help them get this one. We can wait for another."

Dr. Westover was agreeable to that and told his wife that he would call us first thing in the morning. The next morning came early for us, however, and we left before daylight for a meeting at the Seattle Christian School. Then we went on to Tacoma to record a radio program. When the doctor called us, Dad took the call. We were to call the doctor as soon as we got home, regardless of the time. Late that night I returned home alone; Edythe had stayed in Seattle with her family.

When I called the Westovers, the doctor urged me to come

over. Never mind the late hour, he said. This was important and couldn't wait until morning. You can imagine my surprise when he explained their proposition. Would we be interested? I told him we surely were. Very good; he would arrange for the parents and us to sign release papers in the morning. Those four signatures would give us custody of the baby. Dr. Westover would also arrange for us to meet Les Cooper, an Everett attorney, to initiate adoption proceedings.

I went back home and immediately called Edythe, who was shocked to hear my voice in the wee hours of the morning. Had I had an accident?

"No," I blurted out, "no accident. But I have a baby!"

Edythe wondered whether her missionary husband had gotten drunk. I explained the situation as coherently as was possible under the circumstances, and she could hardly wait for the first Seattle bus to bring her back. We were in Les Cooper's office at the appointed time to sign the papers that had already been signed by the adoptive parents. The baby was ours.

The little mite weighed just over five pounds and was considered premature. He would have to stay in the hospital at least ten days, maybe more. That gave us nine days to make the preparations that other parents take nine months to make.

During that time we had to come up with a name. Fantastic ideas presented themselves, but our unanimous choice was Howard Stephen—in honor of Dr. H. S. Westover, who might have been Steve's father. (Incidentally, the Westovers waited a full year before the next baby became available, and they tagged him with the same name.)

Steve was ours at the age of ten days, and we took him home. Never was there such a baby, although he still wasn't ours exactly. The matter of appearing before Judge Charles Denny to hear the magic pronouncement, "Decree of adoption granted," was still a bridge to be crossed.

A social worker came to investigate us. She was young, romantic, and enthralled with our tales of Africa. The idea of world travel was a big factor in her thinking; she was almost as excited about Steve's going to Africa as we were. We knew she would give the court a favorable report.

Our attorney warned us that generally such a case would be held up for almost a year, but he would do his best to expedite matters. He did, and within about three weeks, we were in court with our little Steve, all decked out in the greatest array of flannel and fluff. The attorney stated his case well. The social worker, too, pled for our cause.

Judge Denny was unimpressed, pondering every aspect of the case. His verdict: "After hearing the attorney's statement, and the recommendations of the doctor and the social worker, I will grant the decree for adoption. However, I do so reluctantly, for I feel that if the child grows up in Africa, he will be handicapped in a number of ways."

Then the judge explained that the decree would be an interlocutory decree for a period of six months, after which it would become final. The natural parents could decide to change their minds within that period. If they did, the case would have to come up in court again and be reconsidered.

Bang went the gavel, and out went the parents and the baby. The natural parents, whom we never met, were not at the trial, nor did they know who adopted their child. We remained a bit apprehensive during the interlocutory period, but God's sovereignty decreed that Steve should be ours.

We later went to Judge Denny's chambers to show him pictures of our home in Africa, as well as of Rethy Academy, where Steve would go to school. That relieved the judge's mind, and he admittedly felt easier about his decision. Later, when Steve was six, and on his first furlough, we took him to see the judge. This time he admitted that Africa had certainly not harmed our child.

After our third term came another furlough. This time I was under a cloud. I dreaded another year of deputation meetings, raising money for our return and for another outfit, including a car. But the Lord had a pleasant surprise for me.

Chuck Rall, a member of Bethel Church at that time, was the general director of a sales force that sold "yellow page" advertising for a number of telephone companies in the northwestern states. He wondered if I would like to spend this furlough working for him. There were some disadvantages, since it entailed a good deal of travel and time away from home. But there were also the advantages of a generous salary plus liberal bonuses for extra sales. I could be home each Saturday and Sunday for deputation work. The opportunity was attractive, and after prayer and deliberation I accepted the job.

The experience was new, challenging, and a bit frightening at times. My missionary mentality surfaced, even in that job, and I needed some conditioning. Yet I enjoyed my sales work so much that it actually became a temptation for me to stay on in it and abandon Africa. But, happily, I again became obsessed with the idea that a job was waiting for me in the Congo.

The yellow page interlude was not without its humor. Bill Hehn, another Christian salesman, was not above a prank. He knew that Edythe and I were both a bit strait-laced. After spending a number of days in a certain town, living in a hotel, a number of us salesmen were planning to go home after a few more hours of work. We had our suitcases packed and went to breakfast, but Bill lingered behind a bit. Opening my suitcase, he planted a *Playboy* magazine under some of my folded shirts. He knew that it would be Edythe who would unpack my suitcase.

Imagine Edythe's surprise, and my chagrin, when she discovered the magazine. "Impossible," she cried, "that you would spend our money on such filth."

It was indeed impossible, I retorted; but I had some explaining to do. We both had suspicions that Bill was responsible, and he finally admitted it. Edythe destroyed the magazine forthwith.

Before long, it was time to go back to Africa again. The yellow page experience had been a delightful interlude and just the kind of training I needed for the job that the Lord had in mind for me.

Our furloughs, like those of most married missionaries, have lasted a full year after five or more years on the field. That long a period of course makes it difficult for the mission to find replacements. The optimum would be a shorter furlough after a shorter term of service. But that is not always possible for families, as it means breaking into the child's educational program too frequently. It is also difficult to finance more frequent furloughs. No missionaries get rich during that time. Furlough finances are a bit like golf: one drives his heart out for the green, and ends up in the hole.

(On previous page) Pete and Edythe Brashler. First furlough, 1946.

(Above) Dr. Pierre Marini and his family. He is now director of the Seminary in Bunia.

Director Adriko Adrapi and his family at the Bible School at Adi.

(Above) Reroofing the Adi church. Pastor Yoane Akudri and Roscoe Lee in the foreground.

(Left top) Getting ready for a hunt.

(Left bottom) A 1975 gathering of A.I.M. mission and church leaders. Left to right: Paul Beverly, Norman Thomas, a government official, Wathum, Pastor Balonge, Pastor Pawson, Pete Brashler, Carl Becker.

(Above) Rev. David Pawson with the Brashlers.

(Left) President Mobutu conferred upon Pete Brashler the Order of the Leopard. Here General Lundula presents the medal at a ceremony in Bunia, 1973.

Pete Brashler, now living in Everett, Washington, and serving as Northwest Area Representative for A.I.M.

FOURTEEN
FIELD
DIRECTOR

The Africa Inland Mission field council for the Zaire (formerly Congo) field has always borne a remote resemblance to the United States Supreme Court. The number of men on the council was usually nine. What hair they had on their heads was usually white. There were generally one or two mavericks on the council, too. Like as not, the men were rather forbidding. They had an image that was not to be tarnished, a halo that was not to be knocked awry. According to some new missionaries, the field council presented a formidable front. These men had an aura of infallibility about them; it would never do to question the rightness of their decisions. So they thought, until they got to know them a bit better. They were, after all, quite human individuals whose sense of humor could surface at the least provocation.

These men were chosen annually by missionaries who had been on the field at least one year. Some were allegedly chosen because they treated their wives well. Women were always in the majority on the field, and if they felt that such a man should be their field council representative, then he was voted in. Others were chosen year after year because they happened to be the only eligible man in a particular district. But the majority were voted into office because of the spiritual, professional, and practical contributions they were able to make. They were a good, solid, and sincere group, who commanded the respect of their peers. Frequently, however, they were misunderstood, and for the most part they were a lonely group.

The executive officer of this council was the field director. He, too, was nominated for office by ballots cast by all those who had been on the field at least one year. From among the two or three nominees receiving the highest number of votes from the field, the field council chose the field director. His tenure of office was for five years, and he was eligible for reelection.

Each member of the field council was responsible for the work and welfare of all the missionaries in his district and was also to act as liaison between the African church and the mission. I say *was*, because the field council has become an anachronism. Its authority and importance have declined until it is now only a field committee. The authority the council once had has now been vested in the church council, which consists of both Africans and missionaries, with the former in the majority about two to one.

This bit of organizational background gives an idea of the mission structure under which Edythe and I spent about two-thirds of our career. Our last twelve years or so were spent with the church council being predominant. Under the new regime the church has more to say than the missionaries in making the rules. No longer is the big white *bwana* giving orders. Now it's a team.

It was with a certain amount of hesitancy and reluctance that the A.I.M. accommodated itself to this new setup so urgently demanded by the church. But the African leaders have been patient, and the mission has been progressive enough to make this necessary adjustment. The new African regime by and large is working remarkably well. No system will be perfect this side of heaven, but an organization that is compatible with a strong African nationalism is a must.

Much is heard about a moratorium on missionaries. It is true that the Africans have demanded an end to the old colonial type of mission structure. But with the proper adjustment, and proper church/mission relationship, it is not a "moratorium" they want, but "more-at-togetherness."

This narrative will record what took place historically

under the old field council, as it relates to ourselves. For thirty years the Congo field had a nearly legendary field director named George Van Dusen. He belonged to the colonial era and filled his role well. He was a spiritual father to all our missionaries, who have traditionally numbered 150. He was always the dignified Mr. Van Dusen who shunned first-name familiarity; he addressed each one by his or her proper title.

He was a man of prayer, a very good administrator, an astute businessman, and a rather poor preacher. A man with a razor-sharp sense of humor, he was often hungry for the friendship and laughter so frequently denied him simply because he was the field director. For three decades he served in a job that was difficult and thankless.

Bwana Van, as he was affectionately called, died just before the Belgian Congo was to receive its independence. That left the field without a leader during a very critical period, when unrest, riots, and demonstrations preceded independence. After much prayer and deliberation, Dr. Carl Becker was chosen to guide us through the political intrigue and bloodshed. He, like Mr. Van Dusen, was another lordly and much-loved leader who commanded almost total respect from the family of missionaries.

Already well into his sixties, he accepted the job reluctantly. He would accede to the appointment only if he could carry on his medical work, as he was first and foremost a doctor. But the period was rough, and the field clamored for his leadership.

Independence was granted in 1960. During that year the Congo was convulsed in one crisis after another. Patrice Lumumba came to power, only to be assassinated. There was the secession of Katanga province under the leadership of Moise Tshombe, aided by Belgian mercenaries. The country abounded in natural beauty and natural resources. Potential wealth appeared to be limitless. But the situation was explosive, and we had some 140 missionaries on the field doing their work under chaotic conditions. Dr. Becker was the man to lead us through those stormy seas.

In 1962 Dr. Becker decided that he could no longer continue both as doctor and as director. He felt he must choose one or the other. It was much easier to find someone to re-place him as director than as doctor, and so it was that this "mantle" fell on me. What big boots those were to fill, as the waters were (and would continue to be) even stormier than in the 1960 period. How difficult it would be for anyone to follow two such leaders as Mr. Van Dusen and Dr. Becker.

When the field council meeting at which I was appointed was over, Dr. Becker and I made the long trip to Bunia, driving through the night hours in the moonlight. The road was rough, but the old Plymouth churned along at a reckless rate. We were both weary, and both lost in our thoughts. Dr. Becker's were seasoned with nostalgia; he had enjoyed his work as our leader. My thoughts were steeped in misgivings and apprehension.

Dr. Becker broke the silence as we rode. "Pete, an ex-field director can be a thorn in his successor's side. I am deter-mined not to be that to you. I'm going to disassociate myself entirely from the office, and I will have no advice to offer you. I will be glad to be available for help and counsel when you need it, but you will have to ask for it."

I could have hugged the beloved doctor. I had suspected that this would be his attitude, but it was reassuring to hear him say so. I was glad that at my behest he had been named field director emeritus. Now, after having served in that post for almost fifteen years, I thank God that Dr. Becker has always been available for counsel and encouragement, but also that he has never tried to interfere, or to impose. He is now living in retirement in Meyerstown, Pennsylvania. Re-cently I saw him and reminded him of that night trip and of his promise to me. "Well, I hope I've had sense enough to keep that promise," he said. He has.

Problems presented themselves immediately upon my ap-pointment. There was the case of a promising young man who came with his wife and children to join our staff. They had only recently begun their work of evangelism, stationed by themselves in a remote area. The wife often stayed home with her children for prolonged periods while her husband was out on evangelistic safaris. The long, lonely days and nights of separation made life hard for both of them, but they considered the cost well worth the dividends received in gaining new converts and in building up the church. The pastor and African elders were pleased with this dedicated young couple, and they were deeply loved by all.

Then word came that the husband had had a very serious mishap. He had been overcome by temptation and had committed adultery with one of the young black women.

What a shock! This was such a promising young family, one for whom I had such high hopes. How could the husband have brought such reproach and embarrassment to the Africa Inland Mission, and particularly to the Zaire field? Such was my self-righteous condemnation of this young man.

Another seasoned missionary made the long trip with me to their home. As we drove the endless miles through the forest, we tried to analyze the situation and decide how to deal with the problem. We stopped the car to pray for wisdom. We were baffled, hurt, and disappointed. We became indignant. How could a Bible college graduate, a full-fledged missionary, the husband of a wonderful wife, and the father of three charming children do such a thing? We would certainly have to make an example of him. Our anger grew in intensity as we traveled along.

Our heartlessness turned to confusion upon arrival. We were met at the entrance of the station by a broken young man. In acute shame he greeted us and took us into his house.

There we met the lovely young wife and mother. Her hair was coiffed as though she had just come from the hair dresser. Her dress was stylish and fluffy, and hung gracefully about her. In those days missionary women sometimes had the reputation of "crooked seams"—but not this one. The children were clean, neat, and well-mannered. An ideal missionary family.

How poignant it was. The wife's eyes were too bright; she must have dried away a flood of tears. The husband was full of remorse. As he exchanged glances with his wife, it was obvious that they were still very much in love. These two had come to the field with deep dedication to their Lord and with genuine determination to be high-caliber pioneer missionaries.

What could my colleague and I do? We both felt so inadequate to meet the problem. The first thing I did was to send up an emergency prayer. "Please, Lord, forgive me for the callous attitude I've had toward this young man. Thank you for reminding me of 1 Corinthians 10:12: 'Wherefore let him that thinketh he standeth take heed lest he fall.' Help us to deal with this in love. You take control."

The Lord did, right from the beginning. The indignation we had felt in the car gave way to genuine pity and empathy such as we had never thought possible. With tears of contrition, he told us how in an off-guard moment the Tempter came in with full force and before he realized what was happening, he had committed a deed for which he now hated himself. In one brief interlude his life had been ruined. Or had it?

He had fully confessed to his wife, and been fully forgiven by her. He had wept bitter tears before his Lord. There was no question that his repentance was real. The acrimonious sermon we had prepared in the car seemed totally out of place now.

The young couple looked at us pleadingly. We were reminded of our Lord, when the adulterous woman was dragged into his presence. One by one the accusers had been convicted of their own sin. Jesus, left alone with the condemned woman, asked, "Where are those thine accusers? hath no man condemned thee?"

"No man, Lord."

"Neither do I condemn thee: go, and sin no more."

In the car we had been ready enough to read Psalms 32 and 51, and to be impressed with David's songs of repentance. We could forgive David of his sin, which was far more serious than this young brother's. Now how were we going to deal with the situation at hand? The problem was by no means easy. There were standards to be upheld. What about the Africa Inland Mission's image? Our halo had slipped and fallen into the mud. We were in a dilemma that was difficult and painful for everyone involved.

To meet the immediate problem, we read the two Psalms of David that painted such an apt picture of profound repentance and divine forgiveness. We also read the loving instruction of the aged Apostle John to his "little children" about walking and cleansing and confession. As far as restoration to fellowship was concerned, there was no problem. We would gladly forgive and forget, and be on greater guard for Satan's future onslaughts.

But there was another aspect to the problem. The African Christians knew what had happened. They were strict in disciplining pastors overtaken in the same manner: putting the fallen pastor out of fellowship and relieving him of his pastoral duties.

The church elders were consulted. They, too, wept with us and pled that in this case the missionary should be forgiven. With him it was different, they reasoned. He should not be sent to America; they needed him. God had forgiven him, and why couldn't we immediately reinstate him?

Yet to my colleague and me, and also to the young couple, it seemed incongruous to make a distinction. It was unreasonable to set a double standard. It would sandbag discipline entirely if we made an exception just because the offender was a white man. We must deal with this case just as the Africans did when they had a fallen pastor or elder. The African elders saw the fairness of that position and concurred.

It broke the hearts of the young couple and of all of us. Couldn't we have sent them to the opposite end of the field, or even to another country where A.I.M. was working? But Africa was no longer isolated. News spread fast, with church leaders traveling from country to country. Perhaps later, after a furlough, they could be considered for reinstatement and return to the field. We assured the couple and the church elders that God is a God of grace and forgiveness, but that circumstances demanded that the family be sent home.

My colleague and I were as sad as the young couple were. At least for them the thing was out in the open. The wound was well on the way to being healed. They would start over. Their relationship of love had survived a cataclysmic disaster and was now stronger than before. They believed firmly that God would some day send them back to Africa to do a great work.

Still, my colleague and I felt very much as a father does when he has to punish his child for a gross misdeed; the punishment hurts the father as much as, if not more, than it did the erring child. It was a tremendous introductory lesson for me in becoming the spiritual "father" of our family of missionaries. Discipline was one phase of my work that I would never become callous about.

The handling of such a case invariably draws criticism. There is always a polarization of position, with some inclined to be extremely harsh and others who feel that the offender should be forgiven and reinstated forthwith. I have long since learned that it is impossible to please everybody, but that in all things I must please God and let the chips fall where they may.

There were other problems through the years—not involving sexual immorality, but rather insubordination and recalcitrance. These all had to be dealt with, and very frequently gave us sleepless nights. The handling of such cases, which is an essential part of the field director's role, not only drew criticism but sometimes resulted in estrangement from some of our peers. The path of a leader is a lonely one.

The above story has a happy sequel. The young couple did eventually go overseas again and for years now have been involved in a meaningful ministry of literature distribution and church work. Edythe and I have visited them on a number of occasions, and they are a beautiful family. The marred and broken vessel has been remolded and again put to use. God's grace is great.

FIFTEEN
LIFE
AND
DEATH

"9QAI - ABA is on the air with an important message. Are you reading me, Control?"

"Yes, Aba, you're coming in loud and clear. Go right ahead with your message."

When such a radio announcement was broadcast over the daily mission network, missionaries at all twenty Congo A.I.M. stations alerted themselves. What was the important message coming from Aba?

The speaker was William Stough, a missionary residing at Aba, but not the one who usually broadcast the Aba messages. It was generally Mrs. Coralee Kleinschmidt who gave the Aba news in those days. Could it be that the message concerned Dr. Kleinschmidt, who had so recently suffered a serious heart attack? He had been a guest in our home while attending a meeting of the medical committee. It was touch and go there for several weeks, whether he would survive. But he had recently been making good progress in his recovery and had begun again to make his hospital rounds and to look in on the dispensary. We had heard that only two days ago he had examined all 350 leprosy patients living at the Aba Leprosy Camp. Hadn't he also performed his first emergency operation since his illness? So mused the various ones as they huddled attentively at their radios.

Then Bill Stough's resonant voice came over the air again.

"I have this message to pass on to the field. Dr. Ralph Kleinschmidt left us this morning at 10:30 to join his Lord (April 24, 1964). He sustained a second heart attack as he was shaving, and about four hours later he made his last safari. He is now with his Savior, whom he served so well all these years here at Aba."

The beloved old *munganga* (doctor) was gone. Since coming to Africa in 1923, he had always been ready to go on a medical safari. In the early years he went on foot over hot, snake-infested paths. Under his white pith helmet he called out a friendly *Mbote mingi* greeting to all the Africans he met on the way. He was always ready to dispense medicines or to thump some aching tummy, never failing to leave a word of testimony for his Lord and to point the sick and afflicted to the Great Physician. No night was too dark or rainy, no day too hot or exhausting. This devoted doctor was always ready to heal or to help, sometimes operating under a grass roof with only a kerosene lantern for light.

With the opening of roads in the northeast part of the Congo, Dr. Kleinschmidt began to make his medical safaris by motorcycle. The Africans called this two-legged beast a *pikipiki* because of the noise it made. They howled with laughter as the gentle doctor jumped on the starting pedal and caused the mechanical monster to emit cries of pain, then straddled the thing (much as an African boy would straddle a goat and grab it by the ears) to be carried off with a roar. His amused audience would follow him, imitating the *pikipiki*.

Dr. Kleinschmidt was one of the first missionaries in his part of the Congo to own and use a car. His first one was a shiny black Model T Ford which, after a couple years of relentless use, was replaced by a Ford Model A. That car was likewise doomed to a short but strenuous life as the *munganga* whipped it across rough roads. Always there were the sick who needed his healing touch and the care of Coralee, his R.N. wife, always starched and efficient and tender. Through the years he wore out many an automobile, as indeed he literally wore out himself.

The doctor had received the Savior when he was five years old, and all through his early schooling and later through his medical education and internship, his commitment remained strong. As a young intern, many nurses reportedly set their caps for him. But the *munganga* had other interests. He had a goal to achieve. His sights were on the mission field, not on romance. He wasn't playing hard to get. He was just not gettable.

But one nurse was different. She admired his skill and his dedication to the medical profession, and she noted, too, that he had much higher moral standards than did the other interns.

The doctor was also impressed with Coralee. She was already a supervisor of nurses, and she followed her profession with the same relentless devotion. Dr. Kleinschmidt talked to this supervisor about Christ and shared with her his hope of eternal life. She was impressed by what Christianity had effected in this young doctor's life, and also because it made sense. He led her to accept Christ as her Savior, and from then on their mutual attraction took on a new dimension. Later they married and went to Africa, where they worked together sacrificially for forty-one years.

Now, Coralee would be crushed. It was my responsibility to go to her and take charge of the funeral. After expressing my condolences over the radio, I asked Bill Stough to tell her that I would start for Aba immediately and hoped to arrive by midnight.

We were living at Rethy at that time. I took Stanley Kline, an old friend of the Kleinschmidts, and two others in our little Volkswagen, and started out on the 250-mile trip over bumpy roads. In the meantime Bill Stough and his students would make a casket, and Mary White, the second nurse at Aba, would prepare the body for burial. The funeral was set for ten o'clock the next morning—the longest possible delay, considering the hot climate.

We arrived after midnight to find Coralee asleep. We decided not to disturb her, but to see her in the morning. Before six a.m. we were awake. Crowds of Kakwa and Logo people were on the hospital hill, weeping quietly at the door of the doctor's house. There were no demonstrations of pagan wailing. The African pastor had made it clear to the mourners that the *munganga* was now in heaven with the Lord, and that one day—perhaps very soon—we would be reunited with the doctor in the Lord's presence. But silent weeping continued as the crowd sang hymn after hymn of praise and hope.

As Stanley and I squeezed through the crowd and approached the door, who should meet us but Coralee. She was indeed crushed with grief, but her emotions were contained with dignity, and she was obviously being sustained by God's grace. She was the ever-efficient head nurse. She ushered us into the living room, where the doctor's body was laid out on the davenport. Mary White had performed her mortician's duties well, and the doctor lay as though asleep.

But Coralee did not have much time for us. She was concerned with the tearful crowd who wanted to pay their last respects to their *munganga*. She ushered them in the door in groups of twelve and allowed them to gaze at the remains of their friend for exactly one minute. No more, no less. Then they were ushered out again to make room for the next twelve. This little drama had started at four a.m.

Stanley and I stood quietly by as another group was led in. In this group was the old Kakwa chief. He was a very tall man, dignified and authoritative, but disheveled and clad in old clothes; it would never do to spruce up in such a time of sorrow as this. He laid down his ornamental cane, the symbol of his authority, and knelt down before the doctor who had operated on him several times and who had so often treated him for malaria, hookworm, dysentery, smallpox, and other ailments.

The kneeling chief took the surgeon's hands into his own and began to sob. "Oh, *munganga na ngai* (my doctor), what will I do now that you are gone? I want to go with you into the grave. I was with you in life for over forty years. Now I want to be with you in death."

The chief's elegy would have gone on and on, but his minute was spent. Coralee was in control. She took the towering chief by the elbow and ushered him out. The crowd was growing larger by the minute and the viewing procedure would have continued for days, but at ten o'clock the door was closed promptly. The body was placed in the beautiful casket, and Bill Stough took it to the chapel.

Missionaries from neighboring stations—the nearest ones

over fifty miles away, and those like Aru and Watsa, well over one hundred—were all present for the funeral. This was no doubt to be the most triumphant occasion the Aba station had ever witnessed. More than 6,000 people were in attendance. The nearby Catholic mission closed their schools and medical work and came to the funeral en masse. Schoolchildren, teachers, medical personnel, weeping nuns, and priests —African and European—all filed into the chapel. The seventy Greek merchants in Aba township all closed their stores. Dressed in black and mourning unabashedly, the Greeks also found a place in the chapel. Congolese government officials in formal dress were there, as were several contingents of soldiers with all the military brass to form an honor guard. People came by truck, car, bicycle, and on foot. The big Kakwa chief came again and knelt before the casket, sobbing with grief.

The choir sang, "There's a land that is fairer than day." There were eulogies and an extensive obituary. The Lord had supplied the title and theme of the sermon: "The Munganga's Last Safari." For this trip the doctor was well-prepared. He knew where he was going, and whom he was going to meet. To accompany him, he was to have the very best guide: "My presence shall go with thee, and I will give thee rest" (Ex. 33:14). There was ample provision for the doctor's journey, namely, God's grace and strength (2 Cor. 12:9). There were limitless promises to fortify him. While hearts were sad, yet they were glad. Triumph eclipsed tragedy.

The casket was opened and multitudes of mourners filed past as the choir sang. Faithful pastors—some of whom had been operated on by the doctor, all of whom had been prayed for by him—carried the casket to the waiting truck. The military honor guard stood at attention. Dignified officials stood respectfully by with black homburg hats in hand. The honor guard led the entourage to the cemetery.

The doctor's final resting place was beautiful, surrounded by stately palms and colorful jacaranda trees. It was just below the hospital hill where he had worked so untiringly. There the *munganga*'s remains rest, waiting the Resurrection Morning.

Occasions such as these demonstrate the unity that pre-

119

vailed on the Congo field despite the national chaos. There were many trials and testings, but God's hand was recognized in them all. Through them we have been more closely drawn together.

There was the Saturday afternoon in 1969 when Bob Robinson, then living at Adi, called me to the radio. He had been to Arua (Uganda) that morning, some seventy miles away, and brought back the news that Canon Vallor, one of our retired missionaries from England, had just passed away. There were several other problems that he wanted to discuss after the regular mission radio broadcast. After about fifteen minutes of radio conversation, we signed off.

About one hour later Dr. Becker drove furiously into our yard at Bunia. Something was certainly wrong, because the doctor very seldom drove his car alone any longer. He had sad news. Just a few minutes after our sign-off, Mrs. Robinson had radioed Dr. Becker at the medical center, telling him that Bob had collapsed just after his conversation with me. She explained the symptoms to the doctor, and he readily recognized the attack as a cerebral hemorrhage. Within ten minutes, Bob was dead in his wife's arms. They had tried to call us by radio, but I had already switched mine off. Hence the doctor's twenty-five-mile trip from the medical center to inform us.

The next morning Edythe and I flew to Adi. David Amstutz, the son of our old Adja colleague, had made the casket. He and I transported the body to Aba, ninety miles away, in his station wagon, while the women flew to Aba. The funeral had to be at Aba, where we could have a death certificate signed and where there was an official cemetery at the mission station.

The whole event was poignant. Jean Robinson was marvelously sustained, but she returned to her station and her work grieving and lonely. She suffered much, and the family of missionaries suffered with her. Once again the whole field rallied around the widow to bring aid and comfort.

There was also the Ed Schuit family, who had taken over for us at Blukwa when we left on furlough the first time years earlier. Ed had an electric light generator set up on his back veranda, and each evening he filled the tank with enough gas to run the plant about four hours. When the motor ran out of gas it was time for him, his wife, and seven children to go to bed. This arrangement did not indicate that the day's work and play always ended at ten P.M. Rather, the stringent demands on their budget allowed only so much gas each day.

The Schuits' four-year-old was a precocious child who watched and imitated his dad's every move, including the job of siphoning the lethal gas out of the container into the motor. One afternoon he decided to do the job himself, with the result that his lungs filled with the volatile mixture. Within moments the child was dead. The Schuits have buried a big part of their heart in African soil.

Is this a morbid chapter? Perhaps so, but there are some points worth pondering. When missionaries leave for the mission field, they never know whether they will see their loved ones back home again. They never know what part of the family will be missing at the next reunion. This is a fact of missionary life, as of life everywhere—whether in America or Africa, Boston or Bunia. The important thing is to be in God's appointed place, in his will, when such a moment comes.

It should be mentioned that the fondest hope of many missionaries is to enter the Lord's presence right from the mission field, whether by the rapture, or by death. After spending the greatest part of their lives on the field, and making their most intimate friends there, they want to stay until the end comes. Olive Love's experience illustrates what I mean.

Olive Love lived in Washington, D.C., where she had studied to be a lawyer. The Lord had tapped her on the shoulder for missionary work back in the mid-twenties. She left the profession she had so coveted, and for which her natural abilities had so eminently fitted her. She could have swayed the most formidable jury to her point of view. That, I was to learn by experience.

Miss Love spent more than fifty years working at Blukwa, one of our beautiful highland stations. Her job was to build up an orphanage and a girls' home. She was all business, running the institution with efficiency and dedication. It was strictly a no-nonsense operation, in which she herself saw to the large gardens that produced food for several hundred girls.

Olive was impressed with the delicate basketry that was a product of African culture around Blukwa. She took this native craft and developed it into a lucrative business by introducing new patterns and designs as well as bright-colored dyes to make the baskets more beautiful. The girls learned the new techniques and produced baskets in large quantities. These were sold to Greek merchants in Bunia, to world-traveling visitors, or to tycoon tourists. Olive took the proceeds of this business and plowed them all back into her institution.

In 1976, when Olive Love celebrated her eighty-third birthday, her age was beginning to creep up on her. She became a concern to us, and we felt she should go home. We discussed her physical problem with others at the Blukwa station and with the field council.

I broached the subject with Olive herself, expecting a rather violent reaction. She was getting old, but she still had the old spark of revolution lighting up her system.

"Retire? Me? Never! Certainly not until you provide someone to do my work for me and when I get her properly broken in. Then I'll start thinking of going home. In the meantime, I'm staying put!"

To provide a missionary assistant for her would be out of the question. We were always short on missionaries. The only viable solution to the problem was to turn the whole operation over to the church and let a qualified African take charge of it. But Miss Love wanted a missionary, and no missionary meant that she would stay on until the very last.

Just before Edythe and I left Zaire for the Comoro Islands in March 1976, I broached the subject again. "Olive, you really should go home for retirement. If you stay on, I'm afraid you'll become bedridden, and then you'll require the full-time care of one of our nurses. That would be OK, but we're short on nurses. You should go home, and as soon as possible."

Had it been anyone except this old lawyer, I would have issued an order. But Olive was more accustomed to giving orders than obeying them, and I wanted to avert a crisis with her. Dr. Becker came to my aid and gave the same advice.

Olive finally agreed to go home as soon as she could wind

up her affairs and turn them over to the nurse at Blukwa, who would in turn pass them on to a well-qualified African woman. In the meantime she was getting weaker, and it was increasingly obvious that she should go home. But the thought of it almost broke her heart, and she secretly harbored the intention of going home for treatment and rest, and then coming back. She wasn't going to give up that easily.

She was in the States when we arrived on furlough in the fall of 1976. We saw her in New York, and she had made a remarkable recovery. In fact, she looked very well in her new clothes and with the bit of weight she had gained. She greeted us gleefully. "I'm going back to Zaire in two months' time, Mr. Field Director, and see if you can stop me."

Sid Langford, an A.I.M. official, and I discussed the matter. Edythe and I had to see Dr. Frame for our own checkup. He would also have to give clearance to Miss Love, and I felt it my duty to do a bit of manipulating. Dr. Frame must not give her clearance; she would be a burden to the medical center.

Dr. Frame agreed I had a point and said he would handle the affair. That was in October, and Edythe and I went on to the West Coast. I felt a bit guilty as I bid Olive goodbye, but I felt relieved.

At Christmas we received a letter from Mr. Langford's office announcing that Olive was back in Blukwa. What strings had she pulled to sway her jury?

God's plan is always better than human manipulation. Olive was back at Blukwa for only three weeks when he called her Home. She went to Glory from the Blukwa exit, rather than from the one in Florida where we have our retirement home. This was exactly what that *grande dame* wanted, and God had granted her the request.

Olive Love is buried in the flower garden beside her home. Many thousands of blacks, her special friends, came to her funeral, which was another triumphal occasion. For weeks her friends, ex-residents in her home, members of her orphanage, and thousands of others, made pilgrimages to her grave to pray, thanking God for her ministry and her more than half-century of devoted service. I am glad that God overruled.

SIXTEEN
GROWING
PAINS OF
INDEPENDENCE

The Congo situation was running like a clock, an alarm clock, and we all knew that the alarm would soon go off. The Congolese, as the Zairian inhabitants were called in those days, had been under Belgium's iron-fisted control for seventy-five years, and they were fed up. Other African countries were gaining their independence; why should they continue as slaves?

The Congo is a vast rain forest of 910,000 square miles, covering most of the great basin drained by what was formerly called the Congo River. (In 1971 the name of the country and the river was changed to Zaire.) The great forest is fringed by rich savanna lands that have produced vast quantities of palm oil, coffee, copal, sugar, cotton, and rubber. Mines in the country have yielded a great share of the world's copper, cobalt, gold, diamonds, and tin.

Zaire is one of the greatest sources of the world's uranium and radium. The immense, deep forests furnish some of the world's finest timber. This potentially wealthy country stretches along both sides of the equator and receives an average of seventy inches of rainfall a year. The hot, humid climate induces prolific and undisciplined growth of vegetation.

In the nineteenth century, such a country was a prize trophy for some colonial power to seize. King Leopold II of

Belgium proved to be the winner in 1885, and turned the vast area into his own private fief. Although he became the despotic feudal lord of nearly ten million inhabitants, he called the country the Congo Free State, and by intrigue he gained international recognition at the Berlin Conference that same year. He was a cruel and capricious sovereign for twenty-three years, until international criticism and pressure caused him to turn his private kingdom over to Belgium as a colony.

King Albert was occupying Belgium's throne when Congo became the Belgian Congo. The colonial administration was far more humane than that of the obdurate and brutal Leopold. It had benevolent, as well as malevolent, features. By and large, the Belgians imposed a rigid but righteous paternalistic regime, a regime that accrued great wealth for Belgium but also offered some benefits to the Congolese. The harsh policy of "keeping the natives in their place," however, made the Congolese vulnerable to socialist propaganda. There was no preparation for self-rule, nor any toleration of African participation in their own governmental affairs. During the middle decades of the twentieth century, the Congolese were ready to test their wings of revolution and rebellion.

"Independence" became the watchword, self-government the cherished goal. Few of them knew what independence meant, but they still believed that it must be a panacea for all their troubles. Certain others, better educated and more radical, cherished the idea that with independence they would be able to move into the white man's house, wear his clothes, eat his food, drive his car, sleep with his wife, and actually be served by him. Those delusions seemed bizarre to the whites, but they were real to thousands of Congolese.

Independence came on June 30, 1960. How was it going to affect missionaries? At that time Edythe and I were home on furlough, and we avidly followed the exaggerated media reports. The missionaries there went through the first weeks of post-independence turmoil without too much concern. Probably it would have little effect on them and their work.

Then rioting and fighting broke out, and the first evacuation of A.I.M. missionaries took place in August, about six weeks after Independence Day. Those with families, and those living in troubled areas, decided to leave. Still, most of the approximately 125 missionaries stayed at their posts.

We returned to the Congo around the first of January 1961, leaving America with mingled emotions to go back into that political imbroglio. We felt confident that God wanted us to return. While we were in London the press reported still more turmoil. We received a telegram from some of our relatives: "USE GOOD JUDGMENT. TIME SO UNSETTLED. WOULD LOVE TO HAVE YOU HOME." Yet we felt impelled to go on back to Congo, known by then as the Democratic Republic of Congo.

The sad story of plunder, panic, and bloodshed has been told all too glibly and sensationally by news media that were often poorly informed. No sooner had we arrived back at Adi than we received urgent advice from the American Consul that all missionaries should evacuate.

That was easier said than done. About 20 percent of our A.I.M. staff could not leave because of roadblocks. Others in more isolated areas opted to stay at their posts. But about 70 percent of our staff felt they should take their families out. Our son Steve was seven at that time, so we packed our suitcases and set out for the border.

When we reached the Aru customs post we were blocked by armed soldiers, who forbade us to get near the barrier at the border. We had to obey; they had machine guns trained on us. We argued with the soldiers until about ten P.M., but couldn't budge them. There was nothing to do but drive the fifty miles back to Adi and spend the night.

Early the next morning we took a seldom-used bush path that bypassed Aru. We made the 140-mile trip to Rethy, where we found a large group of our missionaries ready to go into Uganda via the Mahagi border post. More trouble was anticipated there, so we sent to Bunia, the provincial capital, for U.N. troops to lead us out in convoy. About twenty-five of the "Blue Hats," as they were called, arrived in half a dozen jeeps to lead us on our way.

The convoy consisted of about forty-five missionary cars, each one packed with people and personal effects. All had had to leave most of their belongings at their stations, in the care of faithful African pastors. Some were in tears. Congo had been their home for decades, and now they were leaving, perhaps never to return. Never mind the valuables (such as a beautiful silver set given to us by some dear friends in Everett). Material things took on an entirely different value at such a time. After all, they were inanimate things, and replaceable.

It was a tense moment as we gathered for prayer and a final farewell to our faithful friends. Then we were off, with two U.N. jeeps at the lead, two more along the middle, and two at the tail of the long convoy. What a miserable thirty-mile trip it was. Because it was mid-dry season, dust followed each car in great clouds. Cursing Africans lined the road, shouting epithets. We arrived at the border with eyes, nostrils, mouths, hair, and clothes encrusted with dust.

Once again we were confronted with a roadblock and soldiers. No white man was going to leave the country, we were told. Even then, we didn't worry too much. We had the "Blue Hats" along, and they had been charged to give us safe conduct across the border into Uganda. The U.N. troops began to argue with the Congolese soldiers, who outnumbered them about seven to one. The argument was loud, long, and futile. The Congolese were adamant; no one was to leave the country.

That meant that well over 100 missionaries, plus children from Rethy Academy (the school for missionaries' children), were in a tough situation. The soldiers were angry and made jests at us as we cowered in little groups. We were filthy, sweaty, and very hot under the midafternoon sun. But we still had access to the heavenly Father, and our spirits were lifted as we shared our predicament with him.

Bill Deans, a Plymouth Brethren missionary from Nyankunke, was also in the group. In his car he had a supply of colorful Christian magazines that he edited. He invited the children to arm themselves with a good supply of them and distribute them to the soldiers. That did the trick. I can still see Steve and his friends passing out those attractive periodicals, and the soldiers all clamoring for them. They forgot their hostility as they read the articles and enjoyed the photography. We gathered in little groups and began to sing hymns and to witness to them.

But we were still held captive. There was very little food or water among the crowd, and we were beginning to feel the effects of the heat. We wandered over to where the U.N. troops were still arguing with the Congolese officers. We would not be released, we overheard, until they had approval from Bunia. Bunia was 120 miles away, and there was no possible way of getting word back before the next afternoon. We were in trouble.

In the meantime another U.N. jeep drove up with a South African colonel inside. He was angry. Why were these missionaries being detained? They must be released immediately. The colonel jumped out of the jeep with his gun dangling ready at his side. He stomped up to the Congolese captain who was in charge of our captors. It seemed as if a very unpleasant confrontation was about to take place.

The twenty-five U.N. men lined up behind their colonel, and the much larger number of Congolese behind their captain. The latter were all fingering their weapons. If a shot were fired, a deadly battle might ensue. We missionaries cowered along the sidelines, as far away as possible.

The South African colonel was on familiar ground in this tense situation. He was going to do all within his power to avoid a shoot-out, but if it must come he was ready for it. In his Afrikaans-accented French he began to talk to the Congolese captain. He conversed, he cajoled, he cursed, and he finally convinced him that to detain us any longer was pointless.

When that drama was finished it was well past midnight. By the time the customs officials had gone through all of our baggage with a fine-toothed comb, the first roosters were crowing out their welcome of the new day.

The night was behind us, and the nightmare was over. We were welcomed into Uganda, where British and Ugandan officials served us hot soup and coffee, and provided us with water to bathe in. What a relief to inhale Uganda's free air. By now our extra adrenaline was spent, and we realized how thoroughly exhausted we were. What amazed us was how well the children had met this major crisis.

Car by car the convoy broke up, some going north to Arua to rest for a few days, others of us driving on to Kampala (the

Ugandan capital), 300 miles to the southeast. We rested there for two days before proceeding on to Nairobi.

The A.I.M. field councils of Uganda, Kenya, and Tanzania made provision for all of us. Within just a few days, some had gone home for furloughs that were due or near due. Others of us were absorbed into the ministries of those three areas. Personnel are always scarce, but with such a sudden influx of missionaries, it took some doing to get each one assigned to a place in which to live and work. We have always appreciated the gracious way in which A.I.M. missionaries in those countries made room for displaced Congo missionaries.

We were sent to Machokos in Kenya. The John Schellenberg family took us in and gave us a job to do. Mine was a familiar situation: teaching in the Bible school. Edythe taught Bible in the primary school, and Steve was enrolled at Rift Valley Academy, our school for missionaries' children at Kijabe. Our Congo Swahili was quite different from that of the more sophisticated Kenyans, but we could make ourselves understood. The Kenyans were often politely amused at our Congo expressions.

We stayed with the Schellenbergs for seven months, until the end of the school year in mid-July. The friendships that developed with them and with many others during that period were enduring ones.

From reports, the political imbroglio had begun to simmer down in the Congo, and most of our missionaries returned within a couple of months. We were committed to the Machokos Bible School until July, at which time we made our way back. Our little VW bug was loaded. On the roof rack we had a Maytag washer resting upside down. The inside of the car was fuller. It was good to be going back to the land where we had, by then, spent more than twenty-one years. We were needed there.

We arrived at the Congo border about noon and were ready to go through customs in good time. Our first shock was from the immigration official at the border post of Mahagi. We could not enter Congo, we were told, without a special permit from the governor in Bunia.

How were we to get this? The immigration men would have to send a telegram, and an answer could not be expected until the next afternoon. In the meantime we would have to go back into Uganda again and stay there for the night. We were told to be back at Mahagi in twenty-four hours.

Back we came, only to be greeted with the same frustrating news. There was no answer to the telegram. Come back again tomorrow afternoon. So back again through customs and immigration we went, to return to Uganda for another twenty-four-hour wait. That frustrating procedure was to be repeated for seven days.

We were so discouraged by the seventh day that we had decided to go back to Kenya and apply for a transfer from the Congo to that field, if we could not go on through to Rethy this time. But evidently God felt that the testing had gone far enough. On that seventh attempt the Congo officials let us on through. They apparently grew weary of seeing us. They stamped our passports, gave our baggage only perfunctory perusal, and waved us through.

Once again we found ourselves back in the Congo, but this time we weren't quite sure that it was so wonderful. The workers at Rethy were discouraged. Riots and racism were the order of the day. But we were back in the land to which the Lord had called us, and we would serve these people for as long a time as the Lord would allow us.

The work was by no means easy. An affair at Ondoleya underscored that realization. At this village, about ten miles out of Aru, there was a large church. The pastor had been one of our Bible school students some fifteen years earlier at Blukwa. He had been a good student and had showed prospects of being a fine pastor. He started his work at Ondoleya very well, and the church had grown rapidly.

But Bible school graduates and pastors are not immune to political intrigue. This pastor started to listen to the racist propaganda and fell victim to it. He began to believe that the missionaries were all part of a plot to enslave his country to the capitalists and to subjugate the Congolese to imperialism. The missionaries were to be hated and driven out of the land. His preaching became a propaganda program to which his congregation readily responded.

The central church council sent three faithful African pastors and me to try to deal with the situation. Upon our arrival, all Ondoleya met us with shouts and curses: the Africa Inland Mission was but an instrument of the imperialists. They had cheated the church out of many thousands of dollars sent from America to help the African pastors. The members of the central church council were only marionettes, dancing as the capitalists pulled the strings. On and on went the barrage of verbal abuse.

Finally the shouting accelerated to a frenzy. It looked as though fighting was about to break out when the leader of the group shouted madly at the four of us: "Take your Bible, and your lying missionaries, and your Jesus Christ, and get out of our village right now. If you don't, we will kill you!" We got out.

Back in the car, and away from the village, we stopped along the roadside. Never had the Congo looked more beautiful, with the pungent eucalyptus trees in bloom, but I am sure our hearts had never felt more like stone than at that time. Never had we been cursed in such a manner. We had a time of weeping and of prayer. We refreshed ourselves with the words of Jesus: "Blessed are ye, when men shall revile you, and persecute you, and shall say all manner of evil against you falsely, for my sake. Rejoice, and be exceeding glad: for great is your reward in heaven: for so persecuted they the prophets which were before you" (Mt. 5:11, 12).

To rejoice after that hellish demonstration was not easy, but those words had been spoken by Jesus himself. They had to be true. Instead of imprecating the villagers in our prayers, we prayed to God to forgive them, and our souls were refreshed.

We heard no more about Ondoleya for about two years. In the meantime the Simba Rebellion had taken place, and all missionaries had to evacuate. Many of the church leaders and pastors were killed. After the blood-bathed dust of the rebellion had settled, and we were back in the country again, we drove one day to Ondoleya. We were curious, so we decided to stop and pay a visit.

Whom should we meet first but the pastor who had been so bitter about us. He was ashamed when he saw who we were, but he obviously was glad to see us as well. He had a score he wanted to settle. He shook our hands warmly and began to tell us what had happened since we had last seen him. He said that the Holy Spirit had sent conviction to his wicked heart. There had been tears of repentance and public confession on his part, and now he wanted to apologize to us. Many of the former rabble-rousers of the church had likewise repented.

The pastor told us that all the leaders of that infamous riot, staged the last time we were there, were either thoroughly repentant or dead. The Lord had used the rebels to kill those who did not repent, and he had miraculously delivered all of those who had repented. Now the church was again growing and witnessing in the power of the Holy Spirit.

During those two years between the first evacuation of 1961 and the actual climax of the Simba Rebellion, there was much unrest. The most disappointing thing was to see a minority (thank God, a small minority) being duped by the rebels and joining them. Yet most of them had now repented and were restored to fellowship with God and the church.

SEVENTEEN
PRELUDE TO
REBELLION

The climate and natural beauty of Zaire are not to be outdone by any other African country. The people are among the finest of God's fallen race. Some of our dearest friends and happiest memories are those from Zaire. It is a land that holds great promise and is worthy of our best missionary and aid programs.

In tracing the events that took place prior to the Simba Rebellion, I do not want to embarrass the people who shared their lives and culture with us for so many years. However, for the sake of honest reporting, and also to show how foreign forces and ideologies can destroy a wonderful country, I want to record some of our experiences. Those events will reflect attitudes and traits that are foreign to our Zairian friends, but which have been learned from ideologies imported into the country by other elements.

A minority group, comprised mainly of the youth of the country, was duped and led by an outside atheistic system. Responsible Zairians were embarrassed that some of their young people were thus deceived, and they resisted the Rebellion with all their power. Through the many hard trials that the church experienced as a result of this movement, it was purified. God's grace always proved sufficient.

One of the forerunners of the Rebellion was a man I'll call George. George often visited us in our Bunia home and also attended our chapel services. We gave him a special welcome, as we were always happy to have government officials in attendance at church. He told us that he had been converted in the Baptist church at Kisangani, and that more recently he had been attending the Salvation Army. Now, since his transfer to Bunia, he wanted to join our church.

One Sunday I preached on the eleventh chapter of John, and at the close of the sermon I made an appeal: "Lazarus, come forth." George came forth. He wanted to confess certain things in his life, and we were delighted. This *chef de poste*, as he was officially designated, was an important official, and his presence meant much to the church.

He and his wife began to visit us more frequently in our home. At times he and his whole family appeared just as we were about to sit down to a meal, and Edythe readily and graciously set places for the unannounced guests.

At that time we were looking for a house to rent for our secretary-general for the committee on evangelism. Houses were scarce, but George appeared to be the man who could help us. In fact, this was one of the responsibilities written into his job description: looking after the houses that had been abandoned by former Belgian officials. George seemed delighted at the prospect of helping in this matter, and he promised us a rent-free house for our evangelist.

But he also had another proposition to make. He wanted the mission to open a bookshop in Bunia, and he thought the old Socophar pharmacy building would be ideal for this. This seemed to be another answer to prayer. We had a small bookshop near the chapel, but the facility was inadequate. The pharmacy building was ideally located in town, right across from the bank. It would meet our need in every way.

"But," said George, "I would like to meet with your field council to discuss this matter with them."

That presented no problem, as our council would be in session the following week. I invited George to meet with us on Saturday afternoon. I thought we could give him an hour or so to discuss his matter with the council. This would still give him plenty of time to make the three-hour trip from Rethy, where the council would meet, back to Bunia.

But George was not satisfied with a verbal invitation. He wanted a written one that would also include another member of the town council named Wino (this bears no resemblance to the American connotation of winebibber). Wino also attended our church frequently, and I knew him well, so I obliged with a written and signed invitation.

Our field council meeting began on Thursday morning. We would have two and a half days to clear up many of the heavy items on the agenda, and then Saturday afternoon to relax with George and Wino. Imagine our surprise when George showed up at six A.M. on Friday instead, wanting to meet with us then and there. We tossed aside our agenda to meet with our guests. After all, they were going to do a great thing in providing a nice building for the bookshop, and it was to our advantage to accommodate them.

The two officials acted very presumptuously toward the council, demanding a copy of the *ordre du jour* (agenda). After all, they said, they had been invited as members of the council, and it was only right and proper that they know what the meeting was all about. George spoke arrogantly of his own importance as a government official. His demeanor was totally different from what it had been before he had the written invitation.

He told us that he had in his attaché case a very large dossier of complaints against the A.I.M.; that he had come to the council as a trouble-shooter and negotiator between the aggrieved church leaders and the imperialist foreign missionaries. He told us that the dossier had been thoroughly discussed by the provincial authorities in Kisangani, and that there was a very great question as to whether the missionaries would be kicked out of the country or put into prison. In any case, it would be much to our advantage if we cooperated with him and his deputy.

He spent the entire Friday and Saturday haranguing the A.I.M. council. We were a bad lot, and our organizational setup was nothing more than a hangover of colonialism. He demanded an immediate change of our constitution and by-laws. The field director's office was to be occupied forthwith by a Zairian. The field council was to be composed of Zairian members only. Perhaps the missionaries would be allowed to stay, if they would become wholly submissive to the Zairian council.

Some of what he said made sense. The mission had long realized that a closer and more meaningful relationship would have to be forged between church and mission, and mission officials had been in the process of adjusting the organizational setup. But to have the state step in and dictate to us was not acceptable, either to the church leaders or to the missionaries. How were we going to get rid of this character?

George and his friend spent the entire weekend with us. His main grievance was against Rethy Academy, our school for missionaries' children. Starting at first grade level and running through the tenth, it provides a superior academic program. When they return to the U.S., MKs have so many social adjustments to make, and such culture shock to endure, that it's to their advantage to feel a bit superior in the classroom. The best qualified teachers and dormitory staff give their lives to provide the best "home away from home" for our children.

This academy was often a sore spot with many of the Africans. George was very knowledgeable about the situation, and he demanded that the academy be placed under an African director and an African school board without delay. The curriculum was to be completely Africanized and taught in French, and the school was to be open to all African students. Those conditions had to be met immediately, or the school would be closed down.

In no way was the mission ready to meet any of those demands on the academy. The Saturday night session closed at an impasse. George and Wino spent Sunday at the mission with George complaining about the accommodations and food. Wino seemed a bit embarrassed about George's behavior and tried to be pleasant.

Monday morning George appeared at the council again, once more ready to press his demands. By this time the council was thoroughly fed up, and cut him short. We made it clear that Rethy Academy was an American school with the same status as the American Embassy school at Kinshasa. Its *raison d'être* was to provide an American education for children of missionaries, or for anyone else who could meet the requirements, so that they could fit into the American school system on arriving back in the States. If the mission could not continue to operate under its own terms, then we ourselves would close the school. Missionaries with school-age children would leave the country.

George was ready for battle and would have wasted more days in debate and harassment. We told him politely but firmly, "*Monsieur* George, we have other business to occupy our time, and there's nothing more to discuss with you. We are inviting you to leave the council room, as we want to get on with our work."

George waved his written invitation. "*Mais, monsieur,*" he protested, "I am an invited member of this council, and I intend to stay until the meeting is adjourned."

"Very well," was our response. "In that case we'll adjourn right now."

We did not adjourn, but we recessed until George left Rethy station. He was angry, but so were the council members. If this was going to be the attitude of government officials, continuing to work in Zaire would be intolerable. We would negotiate with our African church leaders, but not with the likes of George.

I saw him a few days later in Bunia. He was his jolly old self again, making no mention at all of the fiasco at Rethy. Rather, he wanted to discuss the matter of the pharmacy building and the bookshop. I told him we were no longer interested in opening a bookshop in Bunia. I told him, too, that we had finished our agenda after he had left us, and that Rethy Academy would hold to the status quo.

That George was an advance agent of the Simba Rebellion, there is no doubt. I saw him from time to time, but he no longer attended our church. When the Simbas finally came, he joined wholeheartedly with them. Sometime after we had to evacuate, George was executed. I trust that the faith he had previously expressed in Christ was genuine.

George was not alone in his mischief. Another important-looking Zairian came to Bunia and announced himself as the *ministre des affaires économiques*. We never did learn his name, as he instructed us to call him *votre excellence*. He and his several compatriots caused no little fuss in Bunia. I first met them while shopping in the Bon Marche, one of the larger general merchandise stores. Two soldiers, heavily armed, entered the place and ordered all customers outside. As we were leaving, the minister arrived with several more homburg-hatted bureaucrats, each carrying an attaché case. I was not permitted to linger, but I learned later from the Greeks what took place—not only in the Bon Marche, but in every business establishment in town.

These strangers posed as men from the ministry of finance, and the leader was the minister himself. He had "credentials" to prove it. They pawed through all the merchandise, checking the prices. Many of the costly and scarce imported items of merchandise were confiscated on the grounds that they were contraband. All of the liquor was confiscated and loaded into waiting trucks outside. Outlandish fines were imposed for the most absurd alleged infractions. One Greek was fined the equivalent of $400 because his prices weren't high enough. A certain item, claimed the gangsters, should be selling for 130 francs and the Greek was charging only 125. That was unfair. Another Greek was exorbitantly fined for not having swept his floor properly. Every merchant in town was thus fleeced in one way or another.

The merchants wanted to pay their fines with checks, but nothing doing. Only hard cash would do. If they didn't have the cash they were told to get it *toute de suite* or they would go to jail. When they asked for receipts, the minister scoffed at the idea.

When the fines were collected and the choice items of merchandise were loaded, the imposters were ready to leave town. Case upon case of whiskey, wine, and gin were loaded on the trucks. Bunia officials, however, were suspicious by that time. They arrested the minister, and a long confrontation followed. But the minister was a slick talker and a smooth operator. He opened up several cases of Scotch, and their differences with the police were soon drowned in whiskey.

The matter of the collected fines and merchandise was not a big matter, said the Bunia men. After all, it was the Greeks who were the losers, and who was going to shed any tears over the Greeks. But the whiskey posed a problem. That booze was Bunia booze, and it would have to be consumed in Bunia.

A further compromise was struck by the minister in extending his visit for several days and staging a big party. Hundreds of VIPs were invited, and a large amount of the stolen liquor was consumed. When the police were so drunk that they couldn't care anymore, the minister and his gangsters left town.

Swindlers such as those became commonplace in Bunia. Nor did they confine their shenanigans to the Greeks. Not long after the finance ministry phonies fleeced the merchants, we had a visitor at our home. Edythe saw him on the front porch, and she knew immediately that he was bent on mischief. He had come on a bicycle, which he had leaned against the eucalyptus tree at the foot of the veranda steps. He banged on the front door and shouted "*Kuja sasa!* (come here at once)."

Edythe went to the screen door, which she kept locked. (We had learned the hard way that unwanted visitors might appear inside without an invitation.) When this caller saw her, he immediately began an outburst of verbal abuse. "Why don't you *wazungu* keep up the appearance of your place? Your yard is dirty! I am from the *service d'hygiène*, and it's my duty to see that all of the homes, and the parcels of ground on which they stand, are clean. Yours is filthy, and you must pay a fine."

Edythe was astounded. She looked down at the neatly trimmed bougainvillea hedge. Frangipani bushes stood stately and tall all about the yard, blending their delicate white and pink colors. Dahlias grew in symmetrical array. The lawn about the place was neatly cropped. In the back yard were groves of papaya and banana trees, with scattered avocados. There was nothing dirty about this place. Even the gravel driveway had been swept clean with brushbranch brooms.

Who was this person? Edythe didn't want to open up to him, so she called me from my office. When the imposter (as he proved to be) saw me, he began to breathe heavily and to vent his anger on me. I was to pay a fine of 1,000 francs ($20), or I would go to jail. He produced a large yellow official-looking document.

When I opened the door he wanted to step inside, but I blocked his entry. (I suspected he wanted to case the rooms to see if there was enough wealth inside to make a break-in worthwhile later.) I reached for the document and noted that it was a report form from the telecommunications bureau. There was some illegible writing on it, with a scrawled signature on the bottom. It was obvious that the whole thing was a bluff.

I asked him why the director of the *service d'hygiène* had not stamped the document with his official seal. That made him all the angrier, and he threatened to put me in jail. I wondered how he thought he was going to manage that.

The whole thing was ridiculous, but I decided to play along with him. "I can appreciate the work of your department, and the fact that you want to keep the town clean. If you don't, then surely disease will spread. I will go along with you to your director and pay the fine there. You can ride along with me in the car."

"Oh, but no!" he objected. "I have my bicycle there against the tree. You must pay me the 1,000 francs directly. It won't be necessary for you to go to the office."

"But," I teased, "your bicycle will be OK there until we come back. We shall also stop at the police station. If I pay a fine, I want to get my receipt from the police. The police, too, will be very happy to see that you have done your job. Let's go!"

By that time the angry bluff was over. He looked about furtively, and then with a sudden dash he was off the veranda and onto his bicycle. He was gone, with a shower of gravel flying out from under the back wheel of his surprised bicycle. Needless to say, we saw no more of the "agent" of the hygiene department.

We soon learned to recognize the rogues. The responsible Zairians, our friends, were ashamed that their countrymen would stoop to such tricks. We were sometimes amused and sometimes frightened by them. One never knew when such a scheme would be enforced by violence. But through all of this we managed to keep the best of relations with the government officials.

During those pre-Simba days Bunia was the provincial headquarters of the province, which meant that the governor lived only a few blocks away from us. He was a man by the name of Manzikali from the Logo tribe near Aba. He had known Dr. and Mrs. Kleinschmidt well. In spite of the fact that he had a reputation for ruthlessness, he was a very able administrator and did many favors for the mission.

One day he made a trip to Kinshasa, the capital, where he received a new assignment. He was to move to Lubumbashi, capital of Katanga province, to be the governor there. This was the province that had revolted against the central government under Moise Tshombe. There had been a lot of trouble in this southern area, and President Mobutu thought that Manzikali could straighten things out, using his customary ruthless measures if necessary. We were sorry to hear he was being moved away from Bunia.

After receiving this new appointment, Manzikali was to come back to Bunia for only one day to pack up his belongings and then move to Lubumbashi. Instructions were sent out from the *chef de protocole* that we were to go to the airport to stand in the reception line when our ex-governor arrived. Later that same day we were invited to attend a farewell reception in his honor just before his departure.

On that particular day I was unusually busy with guests who had come to Bunia with certain problems needing urgent attention. I would not be able to go and meet the governor on his arrival, but would try to be on hand for his farewell reception.

At noon we were seated around our dinner table with a number of guests (it was a rare occasion in those days when Edythe and I did not have a table full of guests). We heard the crunch of gravel out in the driveway as a car drove up.

Then we were surprised when someone bounded up the steps and, without a knock, threw open the front door. The next thing we knew, a man was in the center of our living room: Manzikali himself. We were amazed, knowing that he had only these few hours in Bunia. We were also delighted to see him.

"*Non, merci,*" he replied to our invitation to join us at the table. "I am very pressed for time. But I did want to come to see you. You have no doubt heard that I am being transferred to the gubernatorial post at Lubumbashi. That will be a very tough assignment and also a very dangerous one. There will be many people there who will want to kill me. I wanted to come and greet you both in case you cannot come to the reception this afternoon. But more important, I want you to pray for me before I go and tackle this dangerous job."

What an amazing thing, to have this important man come to us and ask us to pray for him. We all left the dinner table and joined him for prayer. It was with great warmth that we prayed for him. After that we had a short visit, and he was gone.

Soon he was in Lubumbashi, trying to deal with smugglers of gold and diamonds, and also with insurgents who were still trying to overthrow the government. Dealing with smugglers was not only a tough assignment for him; it was also a temptation. All too soon, like Elisha's servant Gehazi, our governor friend was also involved in misappropriating some of the loot for his own house. Perhaps we did not pray enough for him.

Manzikali was then reassigned to the capital to become the governor of Kinshasa. That was another step upward. Several years later, Chuck Davis, a professor in our theological seminary at Bunia, went with me to Kinshasa. While there we decided we wanted to visit our old friend, the governor, up in the State House.

We were rebuffed by a secretary who did not like the color of our skin. "Of course you cannot see the governor!" was his sarcastic reply. He wouldn't even let us make an appointment to see him.

As we were about to leave, however, another old Bunia friend appeared on the scene. He was the governor's old *chef de protocole*. This tall, handsome, and athletic man came toward us and welcomed us with open arms. He wanted to hear all the Bunia news. He told us it would be impossible to see the governor that day. He was tied up in a conference. But we could have an appointment to meet him at ten o'clock the next morning.

Ten o'clock sharp the following day Chuck and I were on hand, and we were immediately ushered into the governor's office. There sat our friend in all his splendor, a little more portly than when we had last seen him in our living room and with a little more cotton sprinkled through his hair. But he was the same friendly governor with all his customary charisma.

Chairs were ready for us in his spacious and splendid office. What would we have to drink? It would never do to have his Bunia friends come for a visit and not offer them a drink. He must drink a toast to his old friends of the A.I.M. He suggested a Scotch and soda, but he already knew that we would settle for a coke or orange juice. He had both on hand, and while he sipped his liquor and we our orange juice, we had a very amiable visit. "What about Mrs. Kleinschmidt? What about *ma chère* Madame Brashler? What about Dr. Becker?" He was curious. The governor slapped his glass, ice still tinkling inside, onto the tray.

"Now, what can I do for you, Mr. Brashler?" he demanded. "You are my friend, and I know the work of the A.I.M. You surely must have some needs."

"Yes, we do," was our prompt reply. We had been expecting that question. "You know we have three hospitals in our area, and not one of them has an ambulance. We need three properly equipped ambulances. Can you provide them?"

"Three ambulances," mused our friend. He sat silent for a moment, stroking his chin, gazing at the ornate chandelier hanging overhead. Fingering his empty glass on the tray, he said, "Before I can answer your question, I must have some information. I want to know who is in charge of these hospitals, and who will be responsible for the ambulances. Is Dr. Becker still directing the medical center at Nyankundi? Who is responsible at Aba, and who at Rethy? If you can assure me that these vehicles will be under the control of either an American doctor or an American nurse, then maybe I can do something." (That was a switch from the strong popular drive for Africanization. Every department had to be under an African's control by then, or be ridiculed as a hangover of colonialism. But it happened that, at that time, our medical work was still under missionaries' direction. Since then it has all been placed under African control.)

I assured the governor that the vehicles would be controlled by missionary doctors and nurses. That information prompted a bit more fingering of the whiskey glass and a bit more chandelier-gazing. Then, with a slap of his bejeweled hand on his carved desk, he declared, *"Eh bien*, you shall have three fully equipped ambulances."

That was good news, because we really needed them. We thanked him warmly, inwardly hoping that he would not forget his promise. After more diplomatic chatter and more conviviality over yet another glass of orange juice for Chuck and me, and another highball for the governor, we took our leave. From all appearances the visit was a great success.

A month passed, with no word from the governor about the new ambulances. Another month and, finally, six passed. We forgot about the ambulances.

Almost a year after our visit with the governor, an official drove up from the district office. He came into the house and tossed me a dangling bunch of shiny keys. "Your ambulances have arrived from Kinshasa," he announced. "You'd better come and pick them up before someone steals the tires and batteries."

There were only two of them, but they were brand-new custom-made Volkswagen ambulances. One went to Dr. Becker, and the other to Carolyn Saltenberger at Rethy. The third one, we hoped, would arrive soon—but it never did. Whether it was stolen en route, or whether the governor had produced only two-thirds of his promise, we never did find out. But we have been profoundly grateful for the two, which are still in service after seven years of hard use over roads that are, as the Greeks say, "unbelievable."

There's more to Governor Manzikali's story. He became an official hatchet man for the president and ultimately he overstepped himself in his murderous attempts to keep crime under control. He was arrested, tried, and condemned to die before the firing squad. Each time the execution date arrived, however, he was able through devious devices to get the date postponed. Finally his sentence was commuted. He is free again, but with his wings clipped.

We had many opportunities to witness to our friend, and it looked for a while as if he might have really accepted the Lord. But his later behavior negated this. Perhaps he still has his French Bible, and the seeds planted in his heart will yet come to fruition.

EIGHTEEN
GET OUT
WHILE YOU
STILL CAN

On August 5, 1964, Kisangani (then called Stanleyville) was invaded by Simba rebels under a leader named Mulele. (Simba is the Swahali word for lion.) The sordid story of murder and mayhem that ensued has been well-documented in such books as *111 Days in Stanleyville* by Michael Hoyt and *Out of the Jaws of the Lion* by Homer Dowdy.

Unevangelized Fields Mission missionaries were caught in the midst of the bloodbaths and more than twenty of them lost their lives. Simbas came to each of the U.F.M. stations with large trucks and emptied their granaries and storehouses of all food supplies. They stole the missionaries' vehicles and a short time later confiscated their radio transmitters, making them prisoners incommunicado.

U.F.M.'s last radio transmission was directed to us of the A.I.M. and to any other Americans not yet caught behind that curtain of terror. Al Larson, then U.F.M. field director, announced tersely, "Get out if you still can. You have no idea of the seriousness of the situation. This is different from any previous uprising we have seen."

That didn't sound like Al Larson. He was one of those who had always "rolled with the punches," encouraging his faithful band of missionaries to trust God and to "hang in there." Now he was urging everyone to get out. There must indeed be something different about the current crisis.

We were at Rethy then, which was still peaceful as were all of our other A.I.M. stations. We knew that the situation was tense, but tense situations had become a way of life for us. Besides, Stanleyville was 500 miles away. Surely this rebellion would be quashed long before it could reach us.

Yet Al Larson was not one to push the panic button. His advice could not just be brushed aside. There were 136 missionaries and children in our A.I.M. family in Congo, and if their lives were in danger it was my responsibility to do something about it. Even so, the decision to evacuate was a momentous one to have to make.

Although the actual fighting was many miles away, tension in our area began to mount. Roadblocks were placed at regular intervals, and cars wanting to pass through were harassed and often held up for hours. The required road passes were hard to get. Greeks and Belgians resorted to bribery to get theirs, but missionaries frowned on that. (Even so, in desperation, we sometimes did the same.)

The mission had more than $100,000 deposited in the Bunia Bank, most of which consisted of government subsidies to pay salaries of the African schoolteachers. If we left, we would have to withdraw the money and distribute it to the various schools. Stanley Kline, who was then field treasurer, agreed to go along with me to Bunia one day to do the bank business while I got the road passes for our 136 missionaries.

Our trip from Rethy to Bunia was not too bad. We started at four A.M., heading away from the border and into the troubled area, but there were many delays at the roadblocks. The bank was closed when we got there. Because that meant no business for Stanley that day, we both went to the security police and announced that we needed passes for our 136 workers. The officer in charge thought that a good joke.

"You want 136 passes!" he responded with a loud guffaw. "You can't even have one. We've run out of application forms." He had difficulty controlling his mirth as we tried to talk our way out of a tough spot. Yet, in the midst of that dilemma, we felt the Lord's presence. We knew he would help us.

As the officer continued his laughing, we began to laugh

with him. (There was nothing to laugh about, but we could think of nothing else to do.) Our laughter rather neutralized the hilarity of the man behind the desk. The situation was ludicrous, but according to his book we were supposed to panic. We were by no means reacting according to plan, and this big shot did not know how to cope with us.

I finally asked him if he had just one application form left. He looked at us in a puzzled manner. "Yes, I have one form left," he countered, "but what good will that do? You want 136." We talked him into letting us have the one application form and promised we would bring it back. We didn't tell him that it would be the next day, or he wouldn't have let us take it.

We went to the Bunia mission house, just a couple of blocks away, with the intention of cutting a stencil and mimeographing a supply of the application forms. The missionaries who had worked at Bunia, however, already had gone to Uganda, and we couldn't find a stencil or paper. The only thing to do was to drive to Bogoro, fifteen miles to the south. The missionaries from there were gone, too, but the African education secretary provided a stencil, paper, and ink, and let us use the mimeograph machine. We ran through two reams of paper, which gave us a reserve supply of road passes in addition to those we needed immediately.

It was about nine P.M. when we got back to the Bunia house. Stanley and I worked until the wee hours, filling out the 136 forms. Sleep was slow in coming, and we were up again at 5:30. We wanted to be first at the immigration office to get the necessary signature and seal on the documents. Stanley wanted to get to the bank early, so he, too, could finish his job. Perhaps we could get back to Rethy that evening.

When we reached the immigration office, I saw I was not the only one who wanted to be there early. The place already was crowded. Greeks, Belgians, and Congolese were all clamoring for road passes. The inner office door was closed, and only two at a time were being allowed in.

The Lord was at hand to help. An important army colonel arrived soon after I did. He, of course, would not wait his turn. He was there on urgent business, and people stepped aside to let him pass. As it happened, this military man was a friend of mine. He immediately recognized both me and my predicament. Without another word, he took me by the arm and ushered me into the inner office, right up to the raucous character who yesterday had thought our predicament so funny.

"Here, *camarade*," ordered the military man. "You take care of Monsieur Brashler. He has urgent business back at Rethy." I was astounded, and not a little embarrassed, at such preferential treatment. My Greek and Belgian friends would have to wait for hours. But this was God's doing.

I handed the immigration officer the 136 forms, all of which needed his official seal and signature. He glowered only slightly, as he was afraid of incurring the officer's wrath. Without a word he scrawled his signature on each one. Then bang went the stamp, 136 times. The whole job took only about fifteen minutes. To make him feel better, I gave him about 850 application forms, all neatly printed. That brought a big smile back to his face, as he would now be able to fill out passes for the pressing crowd. He would also collect a fee for himself for each one, although he did not collect one from me.

My job was done and it still was very early. The Lord was providing for us. I again saw the army officer and stepped up to thank him. "*Pas de quoi*," he responded. "But you are not through yet. You must also get the signature and stamp of the army and of the security police on each one." So I wasn't doing as well as I had thought.

The army colonel helped me get the army stamp and signature; no problem there. Now the last hurdle was the security police at the other end of town. The Lord had so marvelously helped in getting over the first two hurdles; surely he would help with the security police as well. It was barely 9:30 A.M., so I figured I would be done by noon. I was hoping that Stanley was doing as well at the bank.

But the security police was an entirely different matter. The crowd was just as big as the previous one but much more hostile. In it there were also many Congolese of the "George" type described earlier. I had no friends in this crowd, at least not any who would risk the wrath of the rabble-rousers on the veranda. Remarks were made about the color of my skin and about imperialist, racist missionaries. For sure, I would get no preferential treatment here.

I stood dejectedly at the back of the line. Periodically, fancy cars which had been confiscated from Europeans drove up. Important Congolese stepped out and walked right through the crowd and into the major's office. Guards opened the doors for them, but the situation for me seemed hopeless.

Then I remembered that the Lord was with me. Again his Word impressed itself upon my heart: "Fear thou not; for I am with thee: be not dismayed; for I am thy God; I will strengthen thee; yea, I will help thee" (Is. 41:10). Thank you, Father. Strength and help were two items I needed badly. That promise gave me courage and boldness. I began worming my way through the crowd, squeezing ahead inch by inch. I had to reach the door of the major's office. The weather was hot, and the smell of rancid sweat permeated the air. Perspiring bodies pressed against mine. I dared not take my hand off the wallet in my front pocket. Progress was slow, but steady.

Hunger was beginning to gnaw at my insides, and it was past noon. There was no food, and no prospect of getting any without giving up my hard-won progress. My throat was dry, my lips were parched. I felt dehydrated, and a splitting headache was beginning to develop. "Be not dismayed. I will strengthen thee. I will help thee." That message came back again and again.

At about three o'clock I was at the door. Although the crowd pressed me against it, the door remained impenetrable. I was no better off than those at the tail end of the line. But the occasional VIP kept coming, for whom the door swung open automatically. A plan was beginning to take shape in my mind.

Another car drove up with three military officers, who got out and headed for the door. Like butter under a blow torch, the crowd melted before them. Guards opened the door, and the three VIPs entered. Only there were four instead of three. One was a disheveled and bedraggled white man, his white hair stringy and wet, his damp clothes clinging to his body.

The guards saw him squeeze in, but he was well into the

room before they could grab him. By the time the door had banged shut, the manipulating missionary was inside, still clutching his bundle of precious road passes. The guards shouted, but he was already at the far end of the room, trying to regain his breath and his composure and to mop the sweat from his brow.

I sorted through the stack of road passes, now damp with sweat. They still seemed to be in the right order. With a prayer for more help, I made my way to the major. He, too, looked bedraggled. He had had a long, tough day, and seemed to be in a menacing mood. It was after five o'clock, time for him to go home. "O Lord," I prayed, "help me to get each of these documents signed and stamped tonight."

"How did you get in here?" demanded the major. I had known this officer, too, it turned out. At one time I had given him a French Bible, which had pleased him very much. I gave him my most appealing grin (I'm sure a very sickly one).

"Oh, *bonjour, mon major!*" I greeted him. The Lord was supplying adrenaline again. "It is indeed a pleasure to see you. How did I get in here? Why, the guards let me in. How else would I be able to get into your presence?" In spite of my attempts, the major was not to be placated with pleasantries.

"You have no business in here, Monsieur Brashler!" he growled. "I should throw you out. What is it you want?"

"Only these road passes stamped and signed by you, *mon major,*" I responded weakly. "There are 136 of them. You will be able to get them done by six o'clock."

The major threw up his hands. "136 passes! *S'il vous plaît, mon révérend,* can't you see how much work I have to do? Look at this crowd. And you ask me to sign 136 passes? Impossible! Step aside!"

He brushed me aside and beckoned to another person to approach his desk. He then dealt with several more individuals, but ignored me. I recalled the promise: "Be not dismayed. I will help."

All this time I hadn't moved from the major's desk, and I could see he was ill at ease. This official was not a bad man. He was just in a bad situation. In better days I had visited him in his office and had prayed with him. The French Bible I had given him was lying within reach on his desk. He had assured me that he was reading it regularly and that it restored peace to his mind.

He eyed me over the top of his spectacles. It wasn't his style to treat a missionary this way. Nor had he forgotten the lesson his old patriarch father had taught him: an aged man with hair the color of manioc flour was to be treated with respect.

"Monsieur Brashler, let me see the documents, please." He looked them over and noticed the signatures of the army colonel and the immigration officer already in place. "Let me use your ballpoint pen," he demanded.

Stamp and sign, stamp and sign—136 times. It was dark when the job was done. The major handed back the stack with a tired grin. He felt virtuous for having helped me. I thanked him profusely, and in turn he smiled and muttered something about being glad to help. Yes, the major was a good man.

Back at the Bunia house, Stanley had almost given up on me. He had hot soup and a nourishing supper ready. We were both exhausted and both profoundly thankful that a trying day was behind us. He had been able to negotiate his bank business, and the money was in his bedroom in a suitcase. We prayed that no burglars would break in, since we were too tired to make the return trip to Rethy that night.

In the morning we headed back, with several cartons of ballpoint pens and some cases of hard candy we had found in the Bunia house loaded in the car along with Stanley's money. My precious papers were carefully stowed away in my briefcase. Thanks to the Lord, we had been successful.

We met roadblocks and barriers at regular intervals on the way to Rethy, but we developed an effective technique to cope with these. As soon as we came upon a roadblock, we jumped out of the car, rushed up to the soldiers, and jammed a ballpoint pen into each one's pocket. Then we foisted several pieces of candy upon them and gave them a hearty handshake with a loud and laughing greeting. This was a new approach, and the gregarious Congolese soldiers liked it. After showing them our road passes and engaging in a bit more banter, we were through. We didn't spend more than about ten minutes at any one of the dozen or more barriers.

The road passes were an answer to prayer, the missionaries declared. I didn't tell them what I had done back there on the major's veranda. Perhaps that was better left unsaid. It was the Lord's doing, and it was marvelous in our eyes.

The following day Edythe and I made the long trip to Aungba and Aru to distribute the teachers' salaries and the missionaries' road passes. The Lord helped us to make this trip in spite of the hostile gangs we passed frequently along the road. At one point a rock was tossed in through the car window. Curses and obscenities were shouted at us, but we kept on going. We prayed there would be no flat tires, and there weren't.

Back at Rethy, on August 22, we received a message by radio that the American Embassy at Kampala would be contacting us at eleven o'clock that morning. At the appointed time the vice-consul's voice came on with this message: "The Embassy strongly advises all Americans in your mission to leave the Congo immediately. Pack lightly, as you may have to abandon your cars and walk through the bush into Uganda. The ambassador sends this message with all urgency."

That appeared to be the guidance we had been asking God for. We had tried not to panic, and didn't want to leave the Congo unless it was clearly indicated by God. But the rebels were pressing in from Stanleyville, closing in on all sides.

I responded to the vice-consul, telling him that although the situation was grave, we didn't want to abandon our people. He reemphasized that things had deteriorated. We didn't have much time if we wanted to get out. He said further that he wanted me to convey this message to all of our missionaries on the one o'clock broadcast and that he would be monitoring it.

We called all the Rethy missionaries together, some thirty of them, to discuss the matter before going on the air. Reactions to the embassy's message were varied. A few tended to panic; a few tended to minimize the gravity of the situation. The majority felt that it was God's will for us to leave. We had nothing to gain by sticking to our jobs, and our presence would endanger the lives of African Christians.

At one o'clock all of the stations were called in. I repeated the urgent message from the embassy. Each station came in and expressed the consensus there. God gave us a great measure of unity in our decision to evacuate.

Then I made the following announcement: "All must make immediate plans to evacuate. Pack lightly and leave your houses and goods in the hands of local pastors. Move out as soon as possible, and in an orderly manner—not in convoy, as this might incite hostility at the border." Then I read Jeremiah 39:17, 18. "But I will deliver thee in that day, saith the Lord: and thou shalt not be given into the hand of the men of whom thou art afraid. For I will surely deliver thee, and thou shalt not fall by thy sword . . . because thou hast put thy trust in me, saith the Lord."

The American consul, listening in Kampala, did not come in with any comment. Apparently our decision and instructions met with his approval. There was a prolonged silence after I had made the statement. Many of the operators sat at their microphones with tears overflowing.

The long silence was broken by Dr. Becker's voice coming over the air waves. "This is Doctor Becker from Oicha," he said in his gentle voice. "Pete, I have a personal question. In your statement you say that all must take immediate steps to evacuate. Does that mean me, too? I could do a lot for our people by staying here alone."

"Yes, Dr. Becker, 'all' includes you," I said. "If you stay, others will want to stay with you." That was hard to say to the beloved doctor. He had always been so right in his decisions. I hated to cross him, but this was important.

After an instant his voice came in again. "Very well, Pete. I believe with all my heart that the decision is right. I only wanted to be doubly sure. We shall make immediate plans to leave." Then the doctor concluded his transmission with the familiar message from Isaiah, "Fear thou not; for I am with thee: be not dismayed . . . I will strengthen thee; yea, I will help thee."

There were no more messages, so we signed off the broadcast. Then began the hurrying and scurrying to get safely across the border. There were three points of exit from Congo into Uganda. Some of our missionaries in the northern section would have to go into the Sudan, others into the Central

155

African Republic (now known as Central African Empire).

The first three cars left on Sunday, April 23. They were held up for twenty-seven hours at the border by drunken officials and soldiers and told that the hated Americans would not be allowed to leave the country. The families slept at the border. Worried? Certainly. But they prayed to the God who had delivered the Apostle Peter from prison. The iron gate that separated Uganda from Congo yielded to God's pressure, and they drove their cars through and on to freedom.

Other missionaries went out the northern exit at Aru and still others through the south, past Oicha and Beni and on to Kasese. Bribes were demanded, and many were harassed for hours. But the road passes paid off.

Within less than a week all 136, with the exception of the Charles Davis family and Coralee Kleinschmidt, were out of the Congo. The Davis family were working at Banjwade, near Stanleyville. Would we ever see them again? We wept as we thought of them. Their story of imprisonment and deliverance has been told by Joseph Theophilus Bayly in *Congo Crisis*.

Coralee Kleinschmidt had been detained at Aba. When the American Embassy sent a plane to rescue her, the plane was fired upon and had to come back without her. After three weeks of living hell, she was smuggled out of the country by friendly Greeks.

We ourselves packed three suitcases and left Rethy under a cloud of depression. It had been our peaceful and beautiful home. All our belongings were stored in the house: wedding presents (those that remained), dishes, silverware. What hurt me most was to leave my several thousand books. They were my friends—and irreplaceable.

God was with us. More ballpoint pens, more candy, and even some monetary bribes assisted us on our way—not to mention the magic road passes. We encountered some harassment and cursings, but we were finally through the border. When we looked back into our beloved Congo, our home for almost a quarter century, all we could do was pray. And weep.

NINETEEN
PICKING UP
THE PIECES

"If only we could get into an invisible helicopter and be flown to freedom."

That was the wistful expression of our son Steve during those final days just prior to the Simba takeover. Living in an atmosphere of hostility for many months had overtaxed all of us both physically and emotionally. The responsibility of making the final decision whether or not to evacuate had been a tremendous burden. Yet we didn't realize how tired we were until we got into the then-friendly and relaxed country of Uganda. What a relief it was to be out of the pressure cooker.

Ugandan customs presented no problems. They waved us through with our meager supply of clothing and personal effects. But immigration procedures were a different story.

When we came back from our previous furlough, we had one passport for the whole family. Money was always a concern, and to get just one was the cheaper way out. When we arrived back in Congo, however, we realized what a mistake that was. The explosive situation there would very likely necessitate a separation, and Edythe and Steve would need their own passport. Although the new passport for them had been easy enough to procure in Kampala, the matter of validating it with proper Congolese visas had been another matter.

When my passport came back, accompanied by Edythe's new one, there was a blotchy black *X* across Edythe's and Steve's pictures, and a bold-lettered "Cancellation" stamped over their part of the photo. Her new passport was invalid in the Congo until we could get the residence visa for it.

I had gone to the immigration office in Bunia, but the office was closed. Where was the *chef d'immigration*? we asked one of the guards.

"*Le chef est fuit!*" he answered with a grin. "He ran off to Uganda, taking all the cash out of the office. He was afraid of the Simbas."

What to do? I was told to send Edythe's passport to Léopold-ville (later renamed Kinshasa) to obtain the visa, but I was afraid to do that, lest the valuable document be lost for sure. I was stumped, but then the "trick" section of my brain began to work. It seemed that some scheme was necessary to get us out of this spot.

I have often hated myself for the scheming dishonest connivances to which I've resorted to get out of tough spots. Yet when one's life seems to depend on trickery, one's conscience becomes unreliable. Many times I've identified with Jacob, who stole his brother's birthright and later collaborated with his mother to trick his old, blind, doting father into giving him the blessing. Ironically, the results of his tricks would have been achieved anyway through God's sovereign design, had this trickster only trusted. And thus I've often felt convicted for my attempts to "help" God, rather than just to trust him.

To "fix" my passport, I took one of our prayer cards, cut the picture on it down to passport size, and stapled it directly over the old passport picture. To an inexperienced eye the alteration was not obvious. But an immigration officer might easily have detected it as clumsy tampering with a United States passport, which could have resulted in a heavy fine, a prison sentence, or both.

I hid Edythe's new passport in my briefcase and handed the tampered one to the Congolese border official. He did not discover the fraud. He was more interested in a bribe than in the legitimacy of the passport.

"Bribe!" I exclaimed to him in mock horror. "Don't you

know that we are missionaries, and that we don't give bribes? We are honest people!" How hypocritical can one get?

In spite of that deceit, the Lord looked favorably upon us, just as he had with Jacob. We were safely past the Congolese border, and I was not in jail. Not yet, anyway. But the Ugandan border was still ahead of us, and those border officials would not be so negligent. Now it seemed as though we really were in trouble, and we stopped the car between the two borders to pray about it.

Isn't God's grace great! He gave us peace of mind, reminding us that honesty was really his way, and that from now on we should resort only to it. Before the Ugandan official had an opportunity to inspect the passport, I poured out the whole story to him, confessing that I had tampered with mine. I explained to him that it could very well have meant death to our whole family had we not gotten out of the Congo, and that this devious device was our only hope.

The Ugandan looked at Edythe's new visaless passport. "No problem here," he confided. "You can get the Ugandan visa for this passport in Kampala." When he saw my document with its telltale tamperings, it was a different story. He showed me the fine print on the back cover, stating that altering or tampering with a U.S. passport is a criminal offense.

"But," the kindly Ugandan smiled, "who wants to be killed in the Congo when he can get off with a prison sentence in Uganda?"

He chuckled as, with his penknife, he unfastened the stapled prayer card picture and tossed it into the wastebasket. Stamping the passport and handing it back to me, he explained that I should tell the American consul why the staple holes were in the page. Had he been the Lord, he might have said, "Neither do I condemn thee. Go and sin no more." The Lord let us off the hook, and we were as thankful as we were relieved.

Some of our missionaries had more difficulty getting out of the Congo than we did. Stanley Kline and Dr. Wilcke were almost the last ones out. The doctor was detained at the border and sent back to Rethy, as the rebels there needed a doctor. Stanley volunteered to go back with him. The following day they left Rethy very early in the morning and made their way back to Bunia. A small U.S. Embassy plane came from Kampala to airlift them, along with a few more whites who could not get out. Then the only A.I.M. missionaries left in the Congo were the Davis family and Mrs. Coralee Kleinschmidt.

The Davises had a grueling experience, being kept under house arrest for three months. Chuck Davis was finally imprisoned with all of the other American male missionaries, including Dr. Paul Carlson.

Chuck was with Dr. Carlson when the latter was killed. Central government soldiers had arrived to take control of Stanleyville (later Kisangani), and there was bitter fighting. Chuck barely escaped, with Dr. Carlson at his heels. He had just scaled a wall onto the porch of a house and turned to give Carlson a hand to pull him over when Carlson's body was riddled with bullets. Chuck and his family, along with the remaining U.F.M. missionaries in Kisangani, were airlifted to Kinshasa on November 24, 1964, three months after we had left.

We lingered for about a week along the Ugandan side of the border to help the many African Christians who had escaped through the bush. These faithful people had fled their homes by the hundreds with Simbas hard on their heels. A great many were killed, but these had managed to get away. Their only crime was that they were Christians—and friends of the missionaries.

Once again missionaries from Congo dropped in on the Uganda, Tanzania, and Kenya missionaries, seeking refuge and a place to work. It was no small task for our hosts and benefactors to make room for us, although by this time they were getting used to evacuations. We were able to rent the facilities of the Hill School in Eldoret where we set up Rethy Academy in exile. The Kenya field council placed the large Eldoret mission house at our disposal. The Klines and we shared the house and set up the field office there. Unfortunately most of our records, except the very recent ones, were locked in my office back in the Congo.

In cooperation with the field directors of the other four A.I.M. fields, we were able to assign all the Congo mission-

160

aries to various useful jobs. Although the Congo field was in exile, it was intact. I shall always be grateful to Erik Barnett, Seton Maclure, Paul Beverly, John Lindquist, and Harold Amstutz for their help in rehabilitating and reassigning our evacuees. Also, the Rev. Sidney Langford, our home director, was most helpful in making funds available.

But the Kenya government was not enamored with the Americans. We were a political embarrassment to them. Soon it was decreed in Nairobi that we were all to take immediate steps to leave that country as well. This was no twenty-four hour notice to leave, but we were told to go as soon as was reasonably possible.

What a disappointment. We had come out of Congo emotionally exhausted, and this news added to the stress. But eviction orders from Nairobi were not to be taken lightly.

It was December 1964, and Edythe and I were in the fourth year of our term. We were more than a little tired. Our eviction from Kenya dampened our spirits, but it was God's way of taking us out of the turmoil and letting us go home for a furlough.

Norman and Naomi Weiss, A.I.M. missionaries who had been studying French in Switzerland, (their immigration status presented no problem, as they had not been among the exiles) were summoned to Kenya to take over my leadership responsibilities. Norman was also to keep an eye on the Congolese situation. Should the rebellion be completely quashed, he would make exploratory trips and arrange for a task force to go back and begin the work of reoccupation and reconstruction.

We went home in December 1964 and were given a hero's welcome. Because the Congo was still hot in the news, we were asked to appear on radio and television programs to give an account of the "Congo confusion." The gorier the story, the better. I fear that we were a disappointment to the news media, as we persisted in telling the whole story instead of focusing on sensational incidents. We didn't gloss over the sordid part, but we also gave the optimistic side.

The church members and their leaders were still hanging in there. Medical work was continuing under mission-trained paramedics. Some of our African nurses were still scrubbing up to take surgical care of strangulated hernias, burst appendixes, Caesarian section deliveries, bone fractures, amputations, *et al.*

But the media specifically, and the public generally, were interested in tales of torture. They listened to our plans for reentry and reconstruction with polite but poorly concealed yawns.

It took us weeks to regain emotional composure. Again and again we related the "Congo story" in churches, only to break down in bitter tears, unable to continue our message. Often at night we awoke from horrific nightmares, in which we relived the reign of Simba terror. People at home could not empathize with us. We had survived an ordeal and now we had to keep reliving it. The bloodier the story of mayhem and murder, the better—and the greater the offering.

Psalms and hymns were a balm. It took weeks before we could sing the doxology, or hear it sung, without blubbering. We just could not tackle "Amazing Grace." And when Lois Dexter sat down at the organ in Bethel Church to play "Jesus, Lover of My Soul," the floodgates of emotion were opened wide. Our beloved African brothers and sisters were still in the midst of the "storms of life." At moments like those we prayed fervently that they might know what it was to "hang their helpless souls on Christ," to rest securely on the bosom of the Lover of their souls.

The first Sunday home I was expected to preach at Bethel. As a prelude to the message, Lois Dexter sang "Surely goodness and mercy shall follow me all the days of my life." I was glad that Edythe spoke before I did, since she is able to cope with her emotions better than I can. That gave me opportunity to regain my composure.

Time is a great healer. After a month or more we were in our usual furlough form: about ten pounds of added weight, as well as again being able to put up with the rat race. Bit by bit news filtered in from the Congo. The situation was scarcely improving. Some of the finest pastors had been killed. Many of the church leaders had fled into Uganda for their lives. The church—which numbered well over 30,000 members at that time—was left with a paucity of leaders, and was floundering. We were desperately needed back there.

It was many months before Norman Weiss and his party could make their initial flying survey trip back to Congo. The news was heartbreaking. It looked as though the missionaries had had their day in the country. We started to think of settling down in the United States.

The First Baptist Church of Marysville, Washington, was without a pastor, and the chairman of the pulpit committee was sure that Congo was closed to missionaries for good. He approached me about the opening.

"You won't be going back to Africa," he began, "and we are looking for a pastor. Would you consider accepting the call to the Marysville church? The church is extending you a unanimous call."

We prayed much about this and consulted with our home director, Mr. Langford. We felt it the Lord's will to accept the call, provided we could be released if we were needed in Africa again. Thus it was that we began a pastorate in a wonderful church. We were extremely happy there.

After seven months, a letter arrived from Norman Weiss. Some twenty missionaries were back in the Congo, he said. The going was tough, but going they were. He stated that the field needed us back as soon as possible so that I could resume my duties as field leader.

Leaving Marysville was another wrenching experience. It had been so easy to become emotionally involved with this congregation. But God had work for us to do in Africa. Once again it was farewells and goodbyes.

The return to Zaire was a traumatic experience. This was a land of such contrasts and paradoxes. It was strange going back to a place where we had been so warmly loved and at the same time so fervently hated; to a land of beauty, yet one that held terrible memories.

Our old house in Rethy was a shambles, completely stripped of our furniture and household effects. Memories of earlier, happier days flooded our hearts as we walked through the place. The doors were broken off their hinges. Glass had been broken out of most of the windows. Remnants of demolished furniture were scattered about. Filth and cow manure were everywhere. Surely this could not be the place we had always kept so clean and orderly.

One little token of God's greatness was still in evidence. Over the dining room door we had hung a little plaque with the text, "Christ Is the Head of This Home." There it still hung—knocked askew, but there nevertheless, bearing witness to the lordship of Christ. We still have that plaque in our Everett home.

The office, too, was a shambles. The filing cabinets had been hacked open, and the mission's files and documents were scattered everywhere, caked with cow manure. And my books. Precious books. I felt about them as the Apostle Paul must have felt about his when he ordered Timothy to come to him in prison. "Bring the cloak," he begged, "and the books."

Here at my feet, filthy and damaged, I found my books. Many of these familiar friends were ripped apart and were beyond repair. Obscenities were scrawled irreverently across some of the pages. An irreplaceable loss.

We felt sorry for ourselves as we set out to clean up the mess and to restore and salvage what we could. But our self-pity was short-lived as we began to talk to the African Christians. The tales of torture and bloodshed endured by our brothers and sisters were unbelievable. Indeed, they "wrought righteousness, stopped the mouths of lions (Simbas), escaped the sword, waxed valiant." Our own losses and sufferings had been told throughout the world. Faithful Christians had upheld us in prayer and later made up our physical losses. They had wept with us and empathized with us over the situation in the Congo. But these dear black Christians had suffered in silence and solitude.

The "Congo Crisis" has been widely publicized, and it is a significant chapter in the annals of modern missions. It is a sordid story on the one hand, but also a thrilling one. It is a story of triumph over sin and death and hell.

We were back, beginning another round of hardship and testings. Hand in hand with the African church, we began to pick up the pieces.

TWENTY
MERCENARY
MENACE

"Hey, Dad, what are all those soldiers doing at the end of the block? They're armed to the teeth, and they look like they're ready for murder. I'm keeping out of their way."

This came from Steve, then twelve. He had just come in from the large manioc garden directly across the street from our Bunia house, where he had been shooting crows with his pellet gun. Crows had declared war on the loquat trees in our back yard, and Steve was out for vengeance. Every crow he shot meant that many more loquats for pie.

As he emerged from the manioc garden he had seen this gang of soldiers. Dismayed, he brought his gun into the house and rode off on his bicycle in the opposite direction.

Steve had not been too keen about the move from Rethy to Bunia. There was always too much activity in Bunia to suit him; he preferred the peace and quiet of a bush station. The field council, however, felt that the field leader should live in Bunia. This town was not new to us, as we had lived there for several years before I was named field director. It had a population of some 60,000, including Africans from several tribes, Asians, Greeks, Belgians, Cypriots, etc.

Bunia was then the provincial headquarters and it was an advantage to be near the provincial offices and the postal/telegraph offices, and to have a bank and airport nearby. One drawback was that any riot or disturbance in the province was bound to originate in Bunia.

Now, soon after our move, the soldiers were beginning to put up a fuss. As Steve rode off on his bike, I returned to my office and dismissed the soldiers from my mind. Only some maneuvers, we figured, and perhaps a few drunks among them.

Soon there was an urgent knock at the door, with much noisy talking. A dozen or more soldiers were outside, and a military truck was in the driveway.

"*Bwana*," the corporal said as I opened the door, "there's an armed mercenary in the neighborhood, and we have orders to capture him dead or alive. Have you seen him?"

So Steve had been mistaken for a mercenary soldier while hunting crows. What a blessing that he had ridden off on his bike, or they would be giving him trouble.

I tried to appear casual. "No, *Monsieur le corporal*," I answered. "The white man you saw was not a mercenary. He was my twelve-year-old son, and the gun he had was only a pellet gun. He was shooting crows."

"*Mais, au contraire, monsieur*," the soldier said. "There *is* an armed mercenary. In fact, there's a whole band of them nearby, and they want to overthrow the government. This mercenary must be found and taken to the captain. Have you seen him?"

My protests were to no avail. I finally fetched the pellet gun to prove my point, only to have it grabbed from me and taken out to the truck. Just about then Steve rode up on his bicycle. The corporal grabbed him, pinioned his arms to his sides, and started to drag him toward the truck.

Steve was stunned with fear, as were Edythe and I. But, like a mama bear robbed of her cub, I was also furious, and I threw myself between the corporal and my boy. In no uncertain terms I made it clear to the corporal that he was making a mistake.

"But *bwana*," protested the corporal, "we have our orders."

"Orders or no orders, you leave my boy alone! If he has to go to the captain, I myself shall take him in my own car. He's not going with you!"

These soldiers were accustomed to obeying orders that were barked out, and my bark was menacing. My anger concealed the fact that I was thoroughly scared. This was before

166

I had received the distinction of the Order of the Leopard mentioned in Chapter 1, or I might have had a little more confidence. Now I had to rely on a loud voice and a hot temper.

Had I been more spiritually mature, I would have relied on the Holy Spirit alone. But God intervened, and the corporal released Steve to my custody.

"But he must come to see the captain immediately," insisted the corporal, "and I must take the 'rifle' with me." Finally the truck roared out of the yard with its boisterous soldiers.

Was Steve scared? You'd better believe he was. But he was a brave boy, and he tried valiantly not to show it.

Before going to the captain's office we took time to read Psalm 46. "God is our refuge and strength, a very present help in trouble. Therefore will not we fear . . . The Lord of hosts is with us . . . Be still, and know that I am God . . ." Then we fortified ourselves with prayer. We assured Edythe we would be back for supper, and off we went in our little VW.

As we drove into the camp we were surrounded by soldiers. They glared at Steve and muttered "mercenary." We ignored the soldiers and found our way to the captain's office. We knocked, but there was no response. We tried the door and it yielded, so we both stepped inside.

There sat the captain behind his desk, thoroughly engrossed in examining Steve's pellet gun. He cracked the barrel to cock it, then took careful aim at an imaginary target outside the window. He squeezed the trigger. "Snap," responded the pellet pusher. He repeated the operation, totally ignoring the scared white-haired missionary and his son.

Finally he relaxed and turned to us with a smile. He beckoned to us to come to the desk and be seated opposite him. I had known this captain for a long time and I liked him. As we sat down, he handed the pellet gun over to Steve.

"*Mon camarade*," said the kindly captain, "here's your gun, and you may take it home with you. What you did in the manioc garden, shooting a few crows, was not wrong. I wish you would kill the whole lot of them, because they destroy so many gardens.

"But, my young friend, you must realize that the country

is in a state of emergency. Our enemies are trying to over-throw the government, and they have hired white mercenary soldiers to help them in their treasonous act. Our soldiers have been ordered to capture all white people with guns. If they cannot take them alive, then they are to shoot them. You are lucky that you weren't shot out in that garden.

"Now take your gun back home," continued the captain, "and leave it there until this emergency has passed. Good-bye, my young friend, and make your aim straight when you start shooting the crows again."

The soldiers were watching this bit of drama through the open window. They had expected an angry confrontation and possibly a beating for the two whites. But the captain was a decent and level-headed man. We left his office in smiles.

The angry demeanor of the soldiers outside immediately changed. Now they all wanted to shake hands with the young "mercenary." This name stuck to Steve for years to come. Even to this day some of the Greeks, when they see Steve, greet him with *"Bonjour, Monsieur le mercenaire."*

During the same period the Greeks operated a cinema, and films were flown in regularly. One was a war picture with scenes of heavy jungle fighting. A special showing of this film was arranged for the Congolese soldiers.

At one point in the film, heavy mortar guns were being fired upon trapped soldiers. This scene was extremely realistic, giving the audience the feeling that they were the trapped soldiers and about to be shot. It was, in fact, so realistic that one of the soldiers shouted *"Vita!"* (which means "war").

The audience panicked and started for the door, but the heavy crowd blocked this point of exit. The only other possible way out was through a large plate glass window, and many of them threw themselves against it.

The theater was a mess. Many of the soldiers were severely cut and had to be taken to the hospital to be stitched up.

The mercenary scare came in 1967. Kinshasa radio announced that a band of heavily armed mercenaries had left Kisangani for Punia, a town in the Kivu spelled exactly like Bunia except for the first letter. But the soldiers in Bunia understood the announcement to say "Bunia." The town went wild.

A military truck, roaring through town, was having a bit of a spark problem in the motor. The timing had slipped, and the truck backfired loudly several times. The marketplace was only a block away from the backfiring, and immediately word spread that the mercenaries was shooting up Bunia.

All hell broke loose. The multitudes in the market abandoned their displays of cabbages, tomatoes, and potatoes, and ran for the bridge that connected the marketplace with their villages. Cows had been slaughtered the day before, and chunks of brisket and broiling meat were abandoned in the market. Fish were left to rot, forsaken by all but swarms of big black shiny flies. Wheelbarrow loads of chickens, trussed together, were left cackling and gasping in the sun. The hawkers ran for their lives. Mercenaries were shooting up the Bunia soldiers.

At the bridge, the only way out of town, there was a war of another kind. Each person was bent on saving his or her own skin, and the fittest survived by edging out the less fit. One mother with a tiny baby managed to get on the bridge. She was brushed against the railing, and her baby was knocked out of her grasp, over the railing, and dashed against the rocks below. Others tried to swim the stream. Many were trampled in the panic as the crowd scrambled away from the backfiring truck.

I had walked to town on some errands that morning, fearing to take our car lest it be commandeered by the army. Military vehicles were scarce. I had learned this the hard way only the day before, when I was out with the car and had it commandeered for the whole afternoon. I finally gained control of it again and drove it into the garage, where I covered it with grass mats. It was locked safely out of sight for the duration.

This morning I found the streets deserted, except for a few rascals who had begun looting. Bunia looked like a ghost town. What desertion and desolation! Village people on the opposite side of the stream were abandoning their homes, fleeing to the hills for safety.

But there had been no more sounds of shooting since early morning. Had the mercenaries been killed, or the Bunia soldiers? Was it a false alarm?

Late in the afternoon Edythe and I decided to walk over to the village. Streams of the morning's refugees were now returning. Some had wheelbarrows loaded with meager possessions. Others carried large bundles on their heads. They were sheepishly opening up their homes again.

Edythe and I greeted them cheerily. Weren't we afraid? they asked. Yes, we had been quite scared. But the scare, we declared, was a false alarm. Further, Kisangani was a long way from Bunia. The mercenaries would surely be killed before they reached Bunia. So cheer up, we encouraged them. God is on our side, and if God is for us, then who are the miserable mercenaries to rise up against us? We shared Romans 8:31 with them.

Our presence meant much to the villagers and also to the officials. We seemed to be a stabilizing influence.

In the meantime Congo was again in the headlines. Our friends and families, worried, began to flood our New York office with frantic letters about the safety of their missionaries. The letters were often scathing, criticizing the mission for not taking decisive action. What kind of heartless bunch were those mission executives, sitting comfortably in the safety of their New York offices while the poor missionaries' lives were in danger?

Another evacuation would be a drastic step to take. This would again mean the loss of each missionary's goods and belongings. Worse than that, it would cause widespread panic among the Congolese as well as among the expatriate population.

Our field council felt constrained to write some reassuring resolutions for the benefit of the discouraged missionaries on the field as well as for the home constituencies. They decided that evacuation was unnecessary at this juncture. Evacuation would cause the African church and the Congolese government completely to lose confidence in the mission. We were to sit tight. Such a "wait and see" policy, as it was dubbed, was deplored by many at home.

By that time the American Embassy at Kampala was also

getting involved. They started to put pressure on us through our mission officials, telling us that staying in the Congo was foolhardy and irresponsible. They kept urging the American officials at Kinshasa to insist on our withdrawal.

Jim Farber was an old-timer at the American Embassy in Kinshasa. He knew Congo perhaps better than any other embassy official had ever known the country. He was also a good friend of ours. Many times he visited Bunia while making the rounds of our stations to enlist the missionaries' help in implementing his relief programs and agricultural projects.

On one such Sunday, after our large church service, we felt rather in the doldrums. Edythe and I were the only Protestant missionaries in Bunia. The airport had been closed for months, so we were getting no mail. Many of our staff were discouraged, and some wondered whether we shouldn't quit and go home. Pressures were mounting. Morale was sinking. It was time to celebrate. We decided to go to the Papanongovich Hotel for our Sunday dinner. Surely a good Greek meal would lift our spirits.

The meal and atmosphere were not disappointing. The Greeks really knew how to put out a lavish spread. As we were enjoying the food and the fun, a huge plane roared overhead. There was excitement everywhere, as there had been no planes for so long. Could this be an invasion? We rushed out to see the huge C-130 fly overhead. There was an American flag painted on the fuselage—a good sight. We decided we would finish our Greek feast and then rush out to the airport to see what it was all about.

Before we finished the sweet dessert, however, an American jeep rolled up at the hotel. The main passenger was Jim Farber, and he seemed as delighted to see us as we were to see him.

"Pete and Edythe," he exclaimed, "you're just the ones I want to see. Do you and your missionaries want to evacuate? We can take a load of you today and get the rest tomorrow."

Evacuate. Imagine! Now our unpanicky pal, Jim, was getting into the act.

"I'm sorry, Jim," I said firmly. "We have no thought of evacuating. We don't feel we're in danger here. The officials are all very friendly and will keep us informed. We'll stay put."

I braced myself for his response. Embassy people can be rough, and to make the long expensive trip from Kinshasa to airlift the Americans, only to be rebuffed, was serious. What surprised us was that Jim Farber wanted to take us out. He had so often spoken appreciatively of the missionaries' stabilizing influence and told us to hang in there. How was he now going to respond to my obstinacy?

"Do you mean that, Pete? Yes, I see you do, and I am greatly relieved at your decision. I, too, feel that it's unnecessary to leave, but you understand the bureaucracy. I was told to come and airlift you. But if you missionaries were to leave, the whole area would go into an unnecessary panic. Since you refuse to go, I cannot force you. But should any of you want to leave, we're ready to take you." I could have hugged the big Yankee.

The Greeks and the Congolese in the hotel were impressed. Imagine the American government taking that kind of interest in its citizens. We were proud of our country, and we had a jolly time at the hotel with Jim and the other Americans. About an hour before sundown they were back in the big awkward bird again, ready to lift it off our unlighted Bunia field before dark.

Our spirits rose. We reported the event to all the missionaries the next day over the mission radio network. It was a great morale booster for all to know that American officials were ready to help when and if needed.

But the mission officials were concerned, too, and wanted to ascertain the situation. A telegram came from Sid Langford, our American home director, informing us that he was making a trip to Kinshasa to meet the American ambassador to Congo. He wanted me to be there. When the field council heard this bit of news they decided that Norman Weiss, deputy field director, should go along on this important mission.

Earl Dix was a member of our field council. He and his wife, Helena, had come to Congo in the mid-twenties and had pioneered the work with the Zande tribe at Banda station. He was an incurable optimist, who not only exuded

172

buoyancy but infected his co-workers with the stuff. He was a guest in our home when Weiss and I were getting ready for our trip to Kinshasa.

"Why don't you take Edythe with you?" asked Mr. Dix. "You'll need her to talk to the ambassador. She's got more common sense than you and Norman put together."

That remark about common sense certainly rang true, painful though it was to a pair of male chauvinists. It would have been great to have Edythe along, but while our exhausted exchequer would pick up the tab for Norman and me, I thought it was entirely unreasonable to expect the field to pay for the "common sense" factor. Our treasury couldn't stand it. I shrugged off Mr. Dix's remark and forgot about it.

But Earl Dix didn't forget. He surmised that my indifference to his suggestion was a money matter. That noon, as we all sat down to the lunch table, there was an envelope addressed to Edythe beside her plate. She opened it, and out fell a card marked "Bon Voyage." Inside was a round-trip ticket to Kinshasa for her. Earl was noted for such generosity.

Edythe went along, as did Bill Deans of the Plymouth Brethren mission. The trip, with the several days in Kinshasa, was a delightful change for us both. Sid Langford was on hand to meet us, and he, too, brought reassurance and encouragement. Sid could always be counted on to be right there in an emergency.

The rendezvous with the ambassador was arranged, and we were ushered into his fancy suite. Mr. McBride was a career diplomat, and he knew his job well. He had been an American ambassador in many lands, and now for some ten years he had been in Kinshasa. He was a man of perception, and he knew what he wanted. In this case he wanted the American missionaries out of northeast Congo. As he saw it, it was an unwarranted risk to leave women and children in that country. Perhaps a few men, yes. But no families.

Again God gave boldness to this little group of missionaries to speak out for his cause. We had learned from Jim Farber that Mrs. Farber was still in the country. We also knew that Mrs. McBride, the ambassador's wife, was still in Kinshasa. We suspected that others on the embassy staff still had their families with them.

We gave a report on the situation at Bunia, indicating that we did not appear to be in any danger of physical harm. Then we posed what proved to be an embarrassing question.

"Mr. Ambassador," we asked, "how many of the embassy families are still in the country?" That elicited an "ahem" and an "ah" or two.

He replied, "Mr. Brashler, I hoped you would not ask that question. It appears incongruous for me to ask missionary families to leave when we still have a number of embassy wives and families in the country. My wife is still with me. I do feel we are safer here in Kinshasa than you are in the Bunia area. Even so, I would rest easier if the embassy families were all out, too."

The ambassador was candid. I didn't like to embarrass this dignified man, but I felt that we knew the situation in northeast Congo better than he did. We explained our position as frankly as the ambassador had explained his, giving him our reasons for wanting to ride out the storm.

"My missionary friends," responded the ambassador, "I cannot order you to leave the country. I can only advise you to go, and that is my urgent advice. I can appreciate your position, and I admire you for wanting to stay. But you must be advised of the danger of a mercenary takeover and realize that such a takeover would mean danger to your personnel.

"I would be much happier if you would go. However, if you stick to your posts, we will be with you in spirit and will do what we can in case of an emergency. But if the enemy takes over, it is highly improbable that we will be able to reach you by plane. May God bless you."

Mr. McBride was not only a diplomat; he was also a sincere Christian. He had transferred his church membership to the Protestant church in Kinshasa, and he had a spiritual as well as diplomatic concern for the country. He was in full sympathy with our missionary program. Later we were honored to have him and his wife in our home as guests. It was indeed a comfort to us missionaries to work in a foreign country with such an ambassador.

The trip to Kinshasa was a success. The ambassador had reassured us. The home director came back to Bunia with us and visited all our stations. Within weeks from the time of

174

the trip, the mercenary menace was effectively dealt with.

Bunia was once again back to normal. Normalcy for Bunia was something quite different from what it would be for a town in the United States, but we were back in business. God had overruled.

TWENTY-ONE
BIZARRE
BUNIA

"Visit you at Bunia! Not if I can help it. I'm giving Bunia a wide berth."

"What crazy new thing is happening in Bunia? If it's new it's got to be crazy. If it's crazy it's got to be in Bunia."

Such is the reputation of our town. Never a dull moment, and seldom a sane one. It was here that Edythe and I spent most of the fourteen years that I was Zaire's field director.

Most of that time Edythe was the busy hostess, receiving many guests each week. It was a role she enjoyed—and filled efficiently. She was the epitome of Paul's injunction, "given to hospitality." When a back problem finally made it difficult for her to continue in this task, it was with much appreciation that she accepted Muriel Davis's offer to take over hostess responsibilities during our last year or two in Bunia.

We were visited by many interesting guests, such as Mr. Lewis Cotlow and his wife. He is a distinguished anthropologist and author (*In Search of the Primitives*), who has made a study of the vanishing civilizations of Africa. He was investigating the famous Duck Bills of the Babira tribe near Bunia. I was able to help him locate them, and we discovered that there were only five surviving Duck Bills.

Mr. Cotlow also made the observation that the Pygmy tribes of the Ituri Forest were the only groups who were not being absorbed by western civilization. Their cultural patterns and life style remain much as they were in the Neolithic era.

Other visitors included famous press agents, *National Geographic* groups, United Nations teams, BBC reporters, and diplomats from the U.S. and Canada as well as from many European and African countries.

But most of our guests were missionaries. Evelyn Kuhnle was one of these several years ago. Shopping and legal business called her to Bunia, and it was my privilege to help her with her legal affairs. Her shopping list took her into the local butcher shop, where she bought bacon, sausage, and other meats, for many months to come.

While she was in the butcher shop, one of the local filchers snatched her purse. That particular purse was a very beautiful one made of bark cloth. Thirty zaires ($60) went with it, not to mention her driver's license, legal I.D. cards, checkbook, and countless other items she could ill afford to lose.

The Bunia police responded to the affair with alacrity and intrigue. "*Bon!*" they cried. "Drive us to the rascals' house, and we will arrest them." Remarkable resolve, this. Had I known where the crooks resided, we would have made a spectacular raid. Knowing their identity would have helped, too.

The officers, however, were not to be outdone by the thieves. Because their police car was *en panne* (as they expressed its broken-down condition), they commandeered my VW and me as its chauffeur. We spent a number of hours combing the city, but with scant success.

Finally they enlisted the help of a less-crooked crook by the name of Mwizi. This fellow generally had one foot on the legal side of the law and the other on the criminal side. The police often used him to elicit information. Mwizi got into the car with us, making six in the little bug. Now we were hot on the trail.

After hearing the report, Mwizi promptly identified the crook as "Jean Bandit" and told the police where to go. The police immediately knew who the character was, but they insisted his name was "Jean Pumbafu" (Jean the fool). In any case, the problem of identity was solved. I was directed to about every bar and brothel in the city. Success was zero, so we started for home.

Near the bridge Mwizi shouted "Stop!" Stop I did, and the less-crooked crook was out of the car with a bound. Threshing through a large crowd, Mwizi grabbed a burly fellow and in a moment had him on the ground. In a few more moments "Jean the fool Bandit" was smothered under a heap of police. A few well-aimed kicks in the head and in the ribs, and the filcher was ready to talk.

That arrest led to the apprehension of five more Bunia thieves, who were all involved. The bark cloth purse, the driver's license, and other legal documents were retrieved, but the $60 was missing. More kicks and the crooks emptied their pockets. Only $20 was left, but Evelyn was happy.

Another friend who often visited us in Bunia was John Strugnell, director of a large general merchandise concern. He was an Irish Catholic, a big handsome man of the world. His sense of humor was characteristically Irish, too.

John went to Monaco for a month's vacation and met a Swedish woman. He knew very little about her except that her name was Irene. He saw her daily during his vacation, and he came back to Bunia engaged. She was to follow in several weeks.

When Irene arrived, John brought her over for us to meet. She was a charming Swede who spoke English but no French. That presented no problem, as John could teach her. He spoke it impeccably, with no trace of Irish accent.

The two were thoroughly in love, and were convinced that marriage was right for them. But there was one problem. Irene was a Lutheran, and as devoted to her church as John was to his. Compromise was simple for John; Irene would become a Catholic. Irene agreed to this reluctantly, but she did want some Protestant participation in the wedding. Would I be willing to assist the Catholic priest?

Me, help a priest perform a wedding? What about my Plymouth Brethren background? What about the Africa Inland Mission? I'd be in trouble with my conscience and my mission. (How bigoted can one get? This was before Pope John XXIII and Vatican II.) But never mind, no priest would want me to cooperate in this wedding, so there was nothing to worry about.

"OK, John and Irene," I replied. "If the priest will come over here and ask me to participate, then I will. But he must ask me, and you know what their attitude toward us is."

"Oh, no problem," the exuberant John assured me. "Just so you are willing."

As I thought through the matter, I could see no reason for being unwilling. My part would be to read some appropriate Scriptures and to offer a prayer. That would not compromise the mission. But why worry? The priest would never ask me.

The priest came several days later on his antiquated Belgian *pikipiki* (motorcycle). A bit embarrassed, he didn't know quite how to broach the subject. "*Mon révérend*," he began at last, "I have an embarrassing question to ask you. It's about John Strugnell and Irene. Will you assist me in marrying them?"

Now I was the surprised one, but I had given my word to the young couple. "*Mais oui, mon révérend.*" But yes, I would be glad to.

It was arranged that the Father would go through the whole Latin ceremony himself. At certain intervals I would read appropriate passages in English and then lead in a prayer.

"Husbands, love your wives, even as Christ also loved the Church and gave himself for it." The last dozen verses in Ephesians 5 would have good advice for the couple, but would also be food for thought for those who attended. Assisting with the wedding would also afford me an opportunity to have a good private talk with John and Irene. Certainly the Lord would be glorified in this, and we would not worry about what critics might say.

The wedding was held in the college chapel at Muji Marie, right near Bunia. There was a good mixed crowd present for it, and everything went off without a hitch. All appeared favorably impressed with this ecumenical ceremony, and it meant much to John and Irene.

To make my part and appearance more fitting to the occasion, I had worn a clerical collar and vest that Edythe found in the attic. I felt silly, and as soon as the doings were over we sped back home. I wanted to divest myself of the clerical collar before any of my peers caught me in it. That was the first (and only) time I had ever worn such garb, and I was extremely uncomfortable.

Imagine my increased embarrassment when we drove up to our house and found a car from Nyankunde in the yard. It was packed full of Plymouth Brethren missionaries, if you please. I was caught red-handed. Could anything be worse? There was nothing to do but to leave the shelter of my little VW and face the music. How would I ever live this down?

Actually, I never did. Those Brethren women have incredible memories, and to this day they remind me with great glee of that episode.

Nevertheless John and Irene were married, and God was glorified in the ceremony. We made many new friends, and the Strugnells have been warm friends ever since.

Bizarre Bunia. Even in the chapel the burlesque could surface at the most inopportune time, such as the Easter morning in the early seventies when I was preaching to an overflow congregation on the glories of the Resurrection. I must have gotten carried away with my subject.

The Swahili word for "Resurrection" is *Ufufuko*. Evidently I put too much wind behind the second *"fu,"* because one of my front incisors dropped on the pulpit with a resounding "ping" and fell at my feet. Embarrassment? Surprise? Shock? All understatements. But I had a sermon to preach, and could not stop.

While I continued to hiss out what I could rescue of my sermon on *Ufufuko* to a sympathetic and embarrassed audience, the song leader was on his knees, scrambling at my feet. He finally retrieved the lost piece of ivory and took it to Edythe in cupped hands. With typical Bantu politeness he curtsied before her and whispered, *"Bwana's* tooth."

Edythe and the rest of the missionaries could scarcely contain their laughter. All of the silly whites were giggling. The Zairian people were just as aware of what had happened as the missionaries, but they all sat in stoic silence ignoring the embarrassing drama. They would laugh about it later, as they sat around their evening meal, but not now to cause the beleaguered preacher more embarrassment.

The offending tooth had been a "devitalized" one (dental

jargon's amazing way of saying that the tooth was dead). The dentist in Nairobi had done a root canal job on it and said that it would be OK for many years. Some days before Easter I had been eating candy (a habit I find hard to kick), and this fragile tooth succumbed to its sweetness.

Our local dentist had cemented a peg in the root, and a falsie on the end of the peg. It had worked fine until I got too excited about Ufufuko. I glued it back with epoxy glue, but it came unstuck periodically. When we got home, our old friend Dr. Baird rooted out the root and built in a bridge.

One Sunday we were invited to participate in a conference at Kasenyi, located on the very hot shores of the lake formerly called Lake Albert. (Recently the president changed the name to Lake Mobutu.) The chapel was filled to overflowing at each of the services.

At the last service sixty-two people were baptized, two of whom were former witch doctors. Both men had an overwhelming fear of water—conditioned, no doubt, by their old belief that spirits dwell beneath the water. The chief sitting beside us declared that this must certainly be the first time either of those men had been wholly submerged. One of the men could not help putting up some resistance, and the pastor had quite a job getting his head completely under water. But the chains of sin had been snapped, and the superstitious fear that had held them for so many years was gone.

The pastor himself gave me some cause for concern, for he was wearing the usual rubber suit with boots attached, to keep his clothing dry during the baptism service. Unfortunately the suit was much too large for him—he looked somewhat like a stalk of celery in an oversized plastic bag. I could see he was in for trouble, because the baptismal tank was too full and the water came much too close to the top of his rubber suit, even though he had it pulled up to his armpits. With the first baptism he shipped what must have been a half gallon of water, and after just a few more the blimp-like suit was completely full except for the volume of water displaced by his own body.

Nevertheless, our attention was riveted on the significant ceremony as it unfolded before us. One of those baptized was a deaf-mute who gave his testimony in sign language. Another was a stammerer. His testimony was spoken with great difficulty, but the joyful expression on his face spoke eloquently of his firm faith in the Lord.

After the baptismal service we were invited to a feast at the pastor's house. At the banquet with us were a number of political and military dignitaries, as well as some leading businessmen. Beside me sat a sergeant-major who had, on a number of previous occasions, given me a bad time. Now, dressed in civilian clothes, he behaved like a gentleman. The head immigration official was there, smartly dressed. He told us that he was a Christian and the son of a Presbyterian minister. The Big Bahema chief across from us ate voraciously. His wife, a former Blukwa girl from our mission school, acted very much the part of a dignified lady. We were proud of her.

Many of the guests of honor were witnessing such a baptismal service for the first time. They were impressed, and it appeared that they sensed their need for God. These people had had their taste of "proletarian government" under the Simba Rebellion, and it had left them thoroughly disillusioned. Now, though once animists, they were hungry for the gospel and began to read Christian literature avidly.

The mood in Bunia in the more sophisticated seventies is largely one of pessimism and fear, bringing the local picture into line with the bleak world picture. Such fear was expressed by the late Bertrand Russell when he observed, "The best we can hope for is unyielding despair." Jesus, too, talked about "people's hearts failing them for fear."

Against the despair of the world the Christian's faith stands in bright contrast. The vigorous African church is fortunate to have strong leadership. Its key people are well-educated, discerning, courageous, and spiritual. They are aware of the total world situation and of Satan's devices. They have the courage to take a stand.

During the dry season of each year, evangelistic teams go out to hold five or six meetings daily. It seems that each year the opposition increases. One official threatened to imprison all the evangelists and trumpet players if they dared to come to his district. But prayer prevailed. When the time for the meeting came, the threatening official was called away by his superiors to answer some charges concerning himself. The meetings were held, and hundreds came to the Lord. Through that season more than 5,000 responded to the gospel invitation.

In 1974 a public execution was staged in Bunia. A local soldier had gone on a drunken binge and slashed a fellow soldier to death. For this he was court-martialed and condemned to death.

Edythe and I went to the big prison where the soldier was being held in maximum security. The man was housed in a little 5′ x 5′ solitary confinement cell, bedbugs and rats his only visitors. Food was shoved to him as though he were an animal.

The corporal wondered why we wanted to talk to such a *nyama* (animal). But if we wanted to talk to him about Jesus, he would see what could be done. We would have to wait while he got permission from the colonel.

Finally the condemned prisoner was ushered into the visiting room. His legs were fastened together with a short piece of chain, secured on each end to steel bracelets riveted around his feet. He could take only about eighteen-inch steps, and in order for him to keep up with the corporal, he had to leap like a kangaroo.

"My friend, I hear that you are going to die before a firing squad," I began rather awkwardly. "Are you ready to die?"

"I'm afraid to die," was his pathetic response. "I don't know whether I killed the other soldier or not. All I can remember is that we had some *gaikpo* (a strong native liquor) and that some of us were fighting over a woman. I woke up in prison, facing a murder charge. Now I must die, and I'm afraid."

We explained to him very simply the way of Life, and he accepted Christ eagerly. Like a drowning man grasping at a straw, he reached out for the Savior. We prayed with him and left him some literature and a copy of John's Gospel, marking certain passages that he should read again and again right up to the end.

We assured him that we would continue to pray for him and that we would surely see him again—if not here in prison, then certainly in heaven. It was with assurance that he hopped back to his cell to await his execution, which might be even the next day.

Later we heard that the death sentence had been commuted and we were overjoyed. But our gladness was short-lived. A few days later, at six o'clock in the morning, the official sound car drove through the streets of Bunia announcing his death.

Whenever a special event was to take place, this jeep with its public address system drove through the streets to herald the news. It drove past our place announcing in both Swahili and in Lingala that our soldier friend was to be executed at the marketplace. Everyone not working at a regular job was to be there to witness the spectacle. Ten o'clock sharp.

Upon hearing this we finished our breakfast in a hurry. I picked up the pastor and we rushed over to the prison. The colonel was already there, and I asked him if we could see the soldier before he was to be shot.

"But he is a Catholic," the colonel objected. "The priest is with him now, administering the last rites. If you want to see him, however, I can arrange it for you."

The colonel ushered me into a little chapel, near the death cell. The priest was there, busy with the Viaticum. It was a solemn setting.

"*Je m'excuse, mon père,*" said the colonel. "The Protestant missionary would like to have a few words with the soldier before you proceed any further."

I was embarrassed. I would have preferred to wait until the priest was finished before starting my visit. But the colonel was also a Catholic, and he realized that the priest would want to have the final words with him.

It was easy to see that the priest was not at all happy with this intrusion, but with good grace he stepped aside as the pastor and I approached the condemned man.

We explained to him again the way of Life, and the soldier responded eagerly. "Yes, yes, I remember what you and Madame told me, and I have faith in Jesus Christ's atoning work on the Cross. I am going to meet my Lord in a very short time, and I am ready."

We read for him the account of the thief on the Cross. "We

185

indeed are condemned justly; for we receive the due reward of our deeds; but this man [Jesus] hath done nothing amiss. And he said unto Jesus, Lord, remember me when thou comest into thy kingdom.

"And Jesus said unto him, Verily I say unto thee, Today thou shalt be with me in paradise" (Lk. 23:41-43).

Then we read the Twenty-third Psalm, and the pastor and I both prayed. Again the convict confirmed his faith in Christ and said that in a short time he would be walking the streets of paradise with his Lord and with the repentant thief. We bade him farewell, but it was only an *au revoir*, for we truly expected to see him again.

The colonel said I would be welcome to go with the soldier to the place of execution, but that it wouldn't really be necessary, as the priest would be there. I was glad to be spared that ordeal.

Minutes after we bade him farewell, the priest finished the last rites. The hapless soldier was led into the truck and whisked off to the marketplace.

Thousands of people were present to witness the execution. There was an air of festivity; it was supposed to be a gala occasion for the crowd. After the shooting, however, the multitudes went back to their homes subdued. They had been reminded in a very dramatic way that death awaits us all. The many rabble-rousers in the crowd had also seen that "the way of the transgressor is hard."

A day or two later I saw the priest in town. I had known him a long time and had been on friendly terms with him. I apologized to him for what he could have considered an intrusion.

"*Mais, pas de quoi, mon révérend,*" objected the priest. "Are we not all brothers? I must tell you that our soldier friend died with great courage. Such bravery! I'm not sure whether it was your prayer and your Twenty-third Psalm, or my extreme unction, or the glass of whiskey the colonel gave him just before taking him out, that caused this man to die so fearlessly. In any case, he died with *bon courage*."

Yes, Bunia is bizarre. Anything can happen. Life there, as elsewhere, is not always sunshine. But in the presence of such grace as we saw activated in the life of the executed soldier, gloom fades into glory. The cloudy days are often the best days to make known the love and forgiveness of our Lord.

TWENTY-TWO
METAMORPHOSIS

Mouvement Populaire de la Révolution is the name of the only legal political party in Zaire. The letters MPR are emblazoned on the national flag beside a flaming red torch, clasped firmly in a raised, clenched fist. The political torch, a symbol taken from the Olympic games, speaks to the Zairians of freedom. This flag flies from monumental towers in every town and village—the banner of authentic Bantu Zaire, a protest against the intrusion of occidental life styles and ideologies.

Founder and president of the MPR, President Mobutu-Sese-Seko, stands foursquare against anything that smacks of imperialism, colonialism, capitalism, or western culture.

Revolution is the hallmark and byword of political life in Zaire. "La revolution" is the theme of the president's popular speeches. It is thought to be the panacea for every socio-economic ill and every political pain. We sometimes get weary of the word. But are we fair to the Zairians when we belittle the revolution?

We Americans feel that revolution is great if it dates back 200 years: the battles of Bunker Hill, Valley Forge, Lexington and Concord; the Liberty Bell; the crossing of the Delaware. How sacred we hold the Declaration of Independence that crushed the juggernaut of British colonialism in our country. This is the glory of American history and heritage. This is the kind of revolution we get thrilled about.

Present-day revolution is different, we rationalize. Traditional patterns of the establishment are being threatened. On the mission field, my "liberties" and "privileges" are being encroached upon. The invincible and infallible field council of the mission is becoming vincible and fallible; indeed, it is becoming obsolete.

Leighton Ford expressed the popular feeling in a discourse decrying racism: "I am no longer able to languish at the 'white' hand of God."

It has been our experience again and again during the past thirty-six years to see the status quo dealt a series of crushing blows. As in America, almost every change has met with resistance in Zaire. When a program is working, why change? But as we have taken a closer look through the eyes of the Zairian nationals, we have seen that the program was really not working very well. Change had to come, and we praise God that the Africa Inland Mission has been flexible enough to adjust.

A.I.M.'s missionary program in Zaire has passed through four distinct stages, and Edythe and I have had a part in each of them. Zaire has moved successively from a colonial regime to independence, to a rebellious takeover by the Simbas, to a reoccupation by the central government, to a military coup, and finally to the present MPR regime under the astute leadership of President Mobutu. Four times the flag has been changed. All of these changes have had their traumatic effects and have often left us bewildered. A.I.M. has had to make adjustments under each regime in order to survive as a mission.

"But," someone asks, "is the survival of the missionary movement a necessity? Isn't it time to call a moratorium on the sending out of foreign missionaries and let the national church take over? Why not give them a go at the helm?"

Perhaps a look at the four stages of our development will help to answer that question. The A.I.M. program was launched during the pioneer period, which eventually gave way to the pastoral period. Then came the parallel period, and finally the partnership period.

The pioneer period began with two apostles, James and John. They were not the James and John of New Testament times, but rather John Stauffacher and James Gribble. John Stauffacher had been in Kenya as a pioneer worker for the Africa Inland Mission since 1903. In 1912 he and James Gribble were ferried across the Semiliki River, which separated the Belgian Congo from Uganda. Through the intervention of President Theodore Roosevelt, who had been a guest at the Kijabe station in Kenya, Mr. Stauffacher had in his pocket a letter from King Albert of Belgium, endorsing the Africa Inland Mission. The letter requested the colonial officials in the Congo to welcome the missionaries and to assist them in getting Protestant mission stations started.

The letter from the king worked miracles. The two white men were cordially received by the Belgian authorities from Mahagi, and permission was given to begin a work for the A.I.M. immediately. The two men, both of whom were suffering from malaria, spent some days surveying the northeast part of the colony. They decided that Kasengu, a place situated in the beautiful hills overlooking Lake Albert, should be the site of the first mission station.

John and James went back to East Africa after the survey. John returned to get his wife, Florence, and their two small boys, Raymond and Claudon, while James returned to the work he had begun in the German colony then known as Tanganyika.

In 1912 (the year of the present writer's birth) the Stauffacher family entered the Congo to begin work among animistic tribes. Mosquitos attacked them day and night and caused repeated malarial attacks, at times in the form of blackwater fever. In those days doctors had no way of effectively treating that deadly malady, and many of the early missionaries succumbed to it, including Peter Cameron Scott, founder and first director of the A.I.M. It has been said that after the first seven years of the mission's existence in East Africa there were more missionary graves than converts.

During the pioneer stage the mission confronted a herculean task. (The account of Jim Bell's entrance into the Pgymy forest is a good illustration of the obstacles encountered.) The Stauffacher family opened the way for the Floyd Piersons, the Earl Dixes, and others to plant the first seeds of the gospel among the large Zande tribe.

John Buyse and his well-educated and refined bride followed the Stauffachers to work among the aristocratic Alurs. John and Helena opened a new station at Ara, and the Alurs' response to that pioneer couple was gratifying.

Buyse was a Dutchman who had served in the Dutch navy. He had been a typical sailor, with a seafaring bent for pleasure and a vocabulary to match. He had a sailor's dexterity in tying knots and in climbing the mast. The life style he had adopted was antithetical to his early Dutch Reformed background. But God had his hand on the young Dutch sailor. While in America, John was saved in a seamen's mission and was later commissioned to go to Africa.

At Ara, John used his nautical expertise in tying knots around the safari loads for the porters. His unusual skill with maps came in handy as he navigated safari groups. Some months after they completed their mud house, Helena had an announcement for her husband—she was going to present him with a new little Dutchman. John was at first incredulous, then ecstatic. In his anxiety for her safety, he wanted to take her to Rethy where she would be near a hospital and a doctor.

"Oh, John dear," objected the bride, who was not only pregnant but pragmatic, "the baby won't be born for another seven months. I'm feeling fine. We can't leave our work now, just as the people are beginning to respond to our message. We're just getting a foothold."

John was only temporarily diverted from his determination to get his wife to Rethy. As the months went by, he often renewed his campaign.

Helena was having serious thoughts about making the long trip. It would take them away from their work for months. They would lose all the ground they had gained. Other pioneer missionary wives had had their babies without medical help.

By the sixth month of her pregnancy, her mind was made up. "John, I have prayed much regarding our baby, and I feel God would have me stay right here for the birth. I don't think it's right for us to leave our young converts. We will remain here at Ara and trust God to help in the delivery."

Her firm announcement touched off a long series of arguments, punctuated by both tears and prayer, but at last John reluctantly acceded to her wishes and on their knees they committed the whole matter to God. The remaining months sped by and John became more and more tender and solicitous of his beloved. Peace ruled in their hearts and home.

When labor began, John felt ready to weather this storm as he had so many storms at sea. But things did not go well; Helena's suffering was almost unbearable, and a whole day passed with no relief—then a second day, and a third. After five days of fruitless labor the exhausted, pain-wracked young woman died.

John Buyse dug his wife's grave right beside their mud house, and tenderly laid her body, with the unborn baby, to rest. He had had his Gethsemane during those five anguished days; now he was able to bring himself to a place of full surrender and pray, "Not my will, but Thine be done."

The work of those pioneers was costly, but it paid lavish spiritual dividends. Several years ago Edythe and I visited Ara. Near the grave of Helena Buyse stood a beautiful chapel, laid up in stone masonry. No missionaries have lived there for many years, but the church is strong. It has withstood the raids of the Simbas and other ravages of Satan.

By 1940 the pioneer period had pretty well passed and was evolving into the pastoral era. Bridges of rapport and communication had been built. The first converts had been won and had to be integrated into the body of Christ and nurtured. That means the translation of the Scriptures into African languages and the beginning of literacy classes. It also meant catechetical classes and the establishment of Bible schools. If the young church was to survive and flourish, it had to have pastoral care.

When Edythe and I arrived in 1940 there were only three ordained African pastors in the A.I.M. church of Congo, which at that time comprised some 15,000 members. There was only one Bible school for the whole northeast corner of Congo, an area of more than 175,000 square miles. The church was young, vigorous, and pulsating with spiritual life, but it needed pastoral leadership. The missionaries were there to provide that.

When we arrived at Adi—as narrated in an earlier chapter

—Yoane Akudri, the national pastor, was there to greet us. The station had been without missionaries for almost a year, and Yoane was overjoyed to have a missionary upon whom he could again lean. During our first day he arrived at our door with cartons of folders, papers, account books, and records. These were the church files that Mr. Richardshon had left in his care almost a year ago.

"These *waragas* (records) are for you, *bwana*," said the pastor. "You are the *Bwana Mokuru* (Big Bwana) of the church. We are seven elders, but we will look to you for guidance."

Had I known what I was to learn later, I would have refused responsibility for those files and insisted that he continue to be the "Big Bwana." But at that time he was glad to foist administrative responsibilities upon me.

It became my responsibility to preach every Sunday morning and at midweek prayer meeting, to chair the meetings of the elders, to baptize believers, and to serve Communion. That was the case at each of our stations where there was a male missionary. The missionary acted as pastor of the church, and the African leaders were content to have it so.

The mission, however, felt that it was wrong for expatriates to retain such responsibilities. Paul's example in Crete was to be our pattern (Tit. 1:5). As Paul enjoined Timothy, "And the things that thou hast heard of me among many witnesses, the same commit thou to faithful men, who shall be able to teach others also" (2 Tim. 2:2).

During the pastoral period the mission's field council set up a council of church leaders, composed of three African elders from each of the five districts and one missionary from each of the three language areas. Thus Jim Bell from the Swahili area, Raymond Stauffacher from the Zande area, and myself from the Bangala area met with the fifteen church leaders three times each year. Through those sessions the church leaders learned how to administer the church.

That stage of the missionary enterprise developed quite naturally into the partnership period. Once the church began to taste the wine of selfhood in the areas of controlling its own government and administering its own finances, it was ready for more. The metaphor of "wine" is well chosen, for it

194

was indeed a joyous occasion when the African Christians took the reins of leadership.

By then the Congolese wanted to sail their own boat. Although they did not want to get rid of their missionaries, nationalism and independence were popular goals.

The mission had to adjust. It was, after all, what we had been striving for: a strong indigenous church. The council of leaders, which had actually been only an advisory committee, and whose actions all had to be ratified by the mission field council, now underwent a metamorphosis.

The name of the new council was to be the central church council. This body of leaders was given complete autonomy in all matters pertaining to mission property and mission personnel. Missionary representatives were to serve on the church council, but no church representatives were to be on the field council.

Missiologist Fulton Darby saw this dichotomous organization as the *sine qua non* for the survival of the missionary movement. Unless the mission's autonomy was retained, he believed, the missionaries would lose a significant incentive for further evangelistic outreach. They would lose all mission and even personal properties, and they would be abandoned to the control of what Darby felt might be a capricious church council.

The African leaders held a different view. To them, this dual arrangement was a two-headed monster controlling the work of the church. It was like two rails on a transcontinental railway running along parallel, in close proximity, but never meeting. Under such a setup there would be lack of unity and resultant suspicion on both sides. The church wanted one council that would control all missionary personnel and all finances. This council would assign and discipline missionaries and approve their return to the field after furlough. All movable and immovable mission properties would be legally transferred to the church.

The mission recognized the need for adjustment, but such an extreme was no answer. Both missionaries and church leaders were unhappy, and it looked as if the A.I.M. work was about finished. We remembered a quote from Thomas Carlyle: "The greatest of faults is to be conscious of none." To the credit of our Zaire missionaries, they were able to gather at our general conference and discuss the issue objectively, without acrimony. It was agreed that, in the light of the revolution and the church's drive for nationalization, radical changes would have to be made. Adjust or adjourn were the two options before us. Mature discussion and prayer were the only methods by which we could handle this crisis issue.

Our mission is organized in such a way that we do not have authority on the field level to make constitutional changes, even in the matters of field policy. We could strive for unity on the field in a given matter, and then we could make our recommendation to the international council.

Unity was not hard to reach. Some of the African church leaders spoke to the general conference, assuring us that they did not want our personal property and were not interested in having our allowances go through the church council. But they did want an organization that would be compatible with the spirit of revolution and Africanization. The proposed parallelism was embarrassing in that it seemed like a hangover of colonialism. They were sure that the details could be worked out in the spirit of Christian love and harmony.

As a result, the conference recommended to the international conference that (1) all mission properties be signed over to the church; (2) all mission departments, such as medical, educational, literature, evangelism, etc., be brought under the control of the church council; (3) all project monies be administered by the church; and (4) missionaries' assignments, furloughs, and discipline be handled by the church council.

It was a historical decision that entailed major and drastic departures from tradition. There were a few misgivings, but with the exception of one negative and two abstentions, the vote was almost unanimous.

Norman Weiss and I took these proposals to the international council. The meeting was held in New York City and it began smoothly, as such meetings usually do. Then came our propositions from Zaire—and the smooth flow of the meeting was sandbagged. What were we trying to do? Sell the Africa Inland Mission down the river?

Long and warm speeches were made, followed by animated

debate. It was thought that Zaire was proposing something far too radical. A vote was taken, and the result was a resounding *No!*

Norman and I went back to Zaire soundly chastened and thoroughly dejected. What were we going to tell our church leaders? How could we face them with this embarrassing news? Face them we must. Missionaries were disappointed when we announced the results over the mission's radio network as soon as we got home. How would the African leadership react to this news?

Upon hearing the results of our New York meeting, the Africans were silent. I waited for an explosion, but it did not come. Pastor Balonge with his characteristic use of analogy said, "If a car is driven down the highway with no brakes, someone is bound to get hurt. We shall accept the I.C. decision as an application of the brakes. We don't want anybody to get hurt, and we have evidently been driving too fast. We shall pray about the issue more, and deliberate more. In the meantime, thanks be to God for giving us mission leaders who are cautious, and who know how to apply the brakes."

Thanks be to God, too, for such maturity. The international council would not meet again for three years, and the delay was a disappointment. During the delay the subject of fusion never died. By the time the I.C. was to meet again, both Africans and Zaire missionaries were more sure than ever that fusion should be given a trial.

The next I.C. meeting was to be held in England, and Norman and I were again delegated to attend. We again prepared our brief carefully. This time there were logical arguments, more stubborn statistics concerning what other evangelical missions were doing, and more prayer preparation. We were ready for the battle, and a bit apprehensive.

Our proposals were again on the agenda and again were discussed in detail. Norman and I had our speeches honed down with formidable facts. We were two "Philadelphia lawyers," prepared for battle.

But the battle did not come. A number of questions were asked, the chairman repeated our proposition, and then a vote was taken. The result: unanimously in favor. We were overwhelmed and overjoyed, even if a bit let down. We had been prepared to fight it out, so the favorable result of the vote was somewhat anticlimactic. We had wanted to argue our cause, but the Holy Spirit had prepared hearts. Now all we had to do was to go back to Zaire and implement the changes.

The task of putting the fine print into our agreement was enormous. Still, we were proud to be part of a mission that had the courage to make changes—not merely for the sake of change, but when conditions demanded them.

In choosing officers for the new organization, the African church showed its confidence in the missionaries by appointing one missionary as vice-president and another as one of the secretaries. As the ballots were passed out for election of treasurer, one of the church leaders got up to make a little speech. "Mr. Chairman, this matter of choosing a treasurer is very important. The money we handle for the church is God's money, and we want to handle it for his glory. We have seen the work of *Bwana* Kline as the mission treasurer for many years, and we Africans have confidence in him. It is my opinion that he should be the treasurer of the new organization."

His speech finished, he sat down. We missionaries sat amazed. We were sure that the rest of the men on the council did not feel that way about *Bwana* Kline. The voting proceeded and the ballots were collected. Result: a 100 percent vote for missionary Kline.

Had we missionaries been guilty of impugning the motives of our black brethren? The procedures of this organizational meeting convinced us beyond all doubt that these men were not interested in fusion for any other reason than finding the best machinery to guide the national church. We whites had reason to be embarrassed about our misplaced suspicions.

The fused organization has now been in existence for almost four years. Fusion has not been the panacea that some expected it to be. The organization is still human, and thus by no means perfect. But it certainly has not precipitated the collapse of the mission's work, as some of the whites expected it to. It is working for Zaire in the present era.

Missionaries are still welcome in the country, and continue to play a significant role. But missionaries who serve there must be willing to identify with the nationals and willing to work under an African council. Illusions of racial superiority will certainly not be tolerated. The ground before the Cross is level.

Such has been our relationship with the church in Zaire. It has been much like that of the Apostle Paul with the Corinthian church, to whom he wrote his epistle "out of affliction and anguish of heart." Often he grieved over them with bitter tears when there were mistakes and defeats. But he rejoiced with them when victories were won.

The country of Zaire and the church there have often been victimized by garbled news releases. Again and again we personally have come to the defense of this militant church when it has been maligned by the misinformation often published in America.

To me it looks as though the big, powerful, political church, like the church of Laodicea in the book of Revelation, will soon be spewed out of our Lord's mouth. May God grant that a large segment of our mission-related churches will be among those whom God loves and chastens; that they will open their hearts' door to his knocking and invite him in to supper.

In chapters 2 and 3 of Revelation, the faithful ones are exhorted to be overcomers, to repent, to hold fast, to be watchful, and to strengthen the things that remain. It is easy enough for missionaries to resign or to withdraw prematurely, but is this what God wants us to do? The only recourse for our church in Zaire is prayerfully and purposefully to resist spiritual decay. The Son of Man is continuing to walk in the midst of the churches and to hold them in his hand. May God grant that both missionaries and their supporting churches in America will stand with the fledgling Zairian church rather than flagellate it through misrepresentation and misunderstanding.

TWENTY-THREE
THE
BEST WINE

"Thou hast kept the good wine for the last." Those words, spoken at the marriage feast at Cana, can be applied to the final chapter in our ministry as overseas missionaries.

Retirement has never appealed to Edythe and me. Gardening, golfing, fishing, playing chess, stamp collecting, are all OK, in their place. But who wants to make a career of them?

Our mission does not compel any of its personnel to return from the field as long as they are physically and emotionally fit. But it does have a definite policy concerning those who hold an executive office, such as that of field director. They are to step down at sixty-five. As I was near that age, my resignation was in order before we came home on our last furlough. Maybe now, we thought, the Lord would let us imbibe some of that "special wine."

Little did we realize that some of it would be savored in the Comoro Islands. We had never heard of them until the meeting of the mission's international council in 1975.

The Africa Inland Mission is always on the alert for new outreach, seeking to penetrate the impenetrable with the gospel. The 1975 meeting of the I.C. had set a goal of recruiting one hundred new missionaries for totally new outreaches in the next five years.

The Comoro Islands have been aptly called the "Treasure House of Perfumes." These four exotic islands are located in the Indian Ocean's Mozambique Channel, halfway between

Africa's east coast and the island of Madagascar (now the republic of Malagasy). They comprise 2,235 square kilometers of volcanic craters and lava flow, as well as large areas of lush green vegetation.

The interest of the scientific world has become focused on the Comoros recently due to the discovery of the famous coelacanth. The first specimen of this rare fish was caught at a depth of 200 meters. Several smaller specimens have been caught since, but it has never been seen in other parts of the world. The fish is famous for its antiquity. Scientists believe the coelacanth to be 300 million years old. It was previously known only through fossil findings.

Little is known of the Comoros prior to the Portuguese occupation in the 1500s. The earliest inhabitants were a Bantu people who established a distinct hierarchical social structure. They were ruled by chiefs who yielded their power to the oldest son of the chief's oldest sister.

The Archipelago has been called "The Forgotten Islands" by some and "The Hidden Islands" by others. However, these interesting dots of volcanic flow and vegetation were not forgotten by, or hidden to, the Muslims. Islamic attention has been focused on them for the past five centuries.

One of the early propagators of Islam in the Comoros was Mohammed Athoumani. His grave is still venerated at Ntsaoueni on the northwest coast of Grande Comoro. It was he, no doubt, who initiated the construction of mosques, along with the reading of the Koran. When Edythe and I stood at his grave, we were impressed with the success of his crusade of the Crescent. How slow we Christians have been to raise the banner of the Cross in its wake.

The estimated population of the Comoros is 350,000. The president himself claimed that the Comorans are 100 percent Islamic. Certainly Islam reigns supreme. Thousands of mosques, with minarets reaching toward heaven, are erected in towns and villages.

It must be noted, however, that a young educated class is far more liberal. They question the traditionally enforced acceptance of the Koran. They have been educated in European schools set up by the French, and many of them have been overseas for university training. They have interacted with the western world and are deviating from the old ways. These younger people, considered apostates in Muslim society, now welcome the presence of Christian missionaries.

About 150 years ago the Comoros came under France's colonial control. In the summer of 1975 a referendum was held to decide the islands' political future. Three of the islands—Grande Comoro, Anjouan, and Mohéli—voted for independence; the fourth, Mayotte, decided to stay under France's political umbrella.

France was reluctant to give independence, but under pressure agreed. Then, feeling that the Comorans were ungrateful for what the colonists had done for them, they withdrew all French doctors, nurses, educators, and engineers.

The islands were left destitute of medical help for the 300-bed hospital el Marouf at Moroni and for all their dispensaries. Secondary schools were paralyzed. The sophisticated electronics equipment at the hospital, radio station, and airport was too complicated for them to maintain. The floundering nation began to look to its neighbors in Africa. Kenya was thriving and prospering; certainly it could help.

So it was that the Africa Inland Mission entered the picture. The Comoran government invited the mission to come over and give professional help. Any missionary with professional expertise was welcome, but it was made clear that they did not want preachers. The Islamic faith was their religion, the Koran their holy book. The A.I.M. was to leave Christianity and the Bible in Africa.

Soon after the invitation was extended to our Kenya missionaries, we met in England for our triennial international council meeting. High on the agenda was the item of the Comoros. There were 350,000 Comorans—totally Muslim; totally ignorant of Jesus Christ as God's Son and our Redeemer. The challenge was tremendous, but what about the restrictions?

Our *raison d'etre* as a mission was to preach the gospel. The professions were used only as a means of getting out the message. How could we justify the expenditure of money and personnel for such an outreach, where our testimony was to be muted?

Our first reaction was negative. But didn't our mandate include humanitarian ministries? Did we have the right to withhold our help when it was within our power to offer it? Our professionals could witness on a person-to-person level. They could show Christ's love by the example of their lives.

Discussion followed debate, but it seemed to get us nowhere. Prayer was our only recourse. After many hours of prayer, God gave us unanimity. We agreed to send professionals to the Comoros. Dr. Dick Anderson, appointed outreach secretary, was to coordinate this work.

Early in 1976 ten of our Kenya missionaries went to the Comoros, including two doctors and their wives, one nurse, one lab technician, one engineer and his wife, one teacher, and one general worker.

At about the same time, we in Zaire held our general missionary conference. The Rev. Norman Thomas, our international general secretary, was present for it. "Pete," he said as he greeted me, "I have an ulterior motive in being here. I've come to tap the shoulders of you and Edythe for the work in the Comoros. Our professionals are there, but they find it difficult to communicate because they are not fluent in French. The officials are suspicious of them. You, with your experience in dealing with government officials, are just the man to get the work started there."

Just a minute, I thought as I mulled over his announcement. This is going too fast. We are to go home in August, and we have a solid program of conferences and meetings before that time.

"Sorry, Norman," I replied. "My successor is still in the States and doesn't expect to be here until August. What about all the conferences?" One just doesn't uproot a field leader on the spur of the moment. The Zaire field, the Zairian church, needed me. I was also thinking about the inconvenience of leaving our Bunia home and the hardship it would be on Edythe. The Comoran challenge was great, but I wished he wouldn't upset our apple cart. Surely some younger fellow would do.

"Yes," he responded thoughtfully, "I realize that you have a big job here. But whether those 350,000 Comorans hear the gospel or not depends on how we respond to this need. We've got to have a leader there now. Would you and Edythe be willing to go if we can provide for your work here?"

"Well, when you put it that way," I replied, "what can I say? Give me the lunch hour to talk and pray with Edythe."

Talk and pray we did. The new job sounded overwhelming. The field would never release us at this stage, nor would the church. So we would agree only on the condition that both church and missionaries would release us—and that just wouldn't happen.

That evening Mr. Thomas shared with the field council the Comoran need and his desire to send Edythe and me over there. Had I talked and prayed with Edythe, and were we ready to go?

I told the council how we felt about it. Should they find a replacement for us, we would be willing to go. But our first responsibility was to the Zaire field. We weren't ready to abandon these people. Both church and mission body would have to agree to our release. That was safe enough to say. I knew they wouldn't be able to find a replacement for us until August.

Once again, pragmatism prevailed over idealism. Earl Dix put it in these words: "Let that opportunity go down the drain just for the lack of a couple to lead a work? Never. We have a responsibility. Sure, we can keep Pete busy here until August, but he's not indispensable. Norman Weiss, the deputy, can take over until the new F.D. arrives. Pete and Edythe can go to the Comoros."

I was stunned. Were these the words of a friend? Would they dispense with a field director that easily? Alas, the other council members concurred. They were all enthusiastic about the new outreach, just as we had been until it began to uproot *us*.

I shared the outcome of the meeting with Edythe later that night. She, too, was jarred. Her arthritic back had bothered her a great deal during this term, and she felt that a move now might be too much. "But cheer up, dear heart," she told me. "The missionary committee might release us, but the church council won't let us go."

The next day Mr. Thomas met with the church leaders. They, too, were impressed with the tremendous need in the

Comoros. "But," objected Pastor Balonge, president of the 90,000-member Zairian church, "we have a program that will take *Bwana* and Madame right up to the time of their furlough. We want them to visit every section of the church. Can't the Comoran job wait until then?"

"Can't wait," replied Mr. Thomas.

The church leaders said some nice things about our thirty-six years in Zaire, and there were expressions of love and appreciation. They hated to see us go. "But," continued the venerable Balonge, "this is God's doing, and who are we to interfere? *Bwana* and Madame will go to the Comoros, and we will go with them in our prayers."

OK, God, we thought. If this is your doing, then we don't want to interfere. After prayer, and a few loud honks into our handkerchiefs, Edythe and I were ready to agree to the idea.

It took us some weeks to turn things over to Norman Weiss and to make several last safaris. By early March, after a round of farewell functions, we were set to go. But to leave Bunia for the last time was tougher than we cared to say.

A Cessna 185 took us to Nairobi. From Nairobi a two-engine Cessna flew us across the blue brilliance of the Indian Ocean. It felt strange to be on our way to a Muslim country— to a people who agreed when Christians talked about the God of holiness, righteousness, and majesty, but who knew nothing about the Father God of mercy and grace. Koranic writings included many psalms, but "like as a father pitieth his children" was not one of them. As we flew we were busy with books on how to witness to Muslims. We were apprehensive, as we had had almost no experience with Muslims.

As our little two-engine bird winged its way eastward, we spotted the tiny dots in the sea that were the Comoro Islands. Our flight brought us to the northern tip of Grande Comoro, the largest island of the Archipelago. The pilot changed to a southern course, following the west coast. Gigantic waves dashed against the volcanic shores, turning the magnificent splendor of the deep blue sea into a mass of foam and spray.

Moroni, the capital, reached out to us, beckoning to us to come and share something with the Comorans. It reminded us of the needy friend in one of Jesus' parables who reached out for something in the course of his midnight journey. "Friend, lend me three loaves."

Moroni had reached out to Islam, only to be disappointed. "I have nothing to set before you."

It had reached out to political independence, only to be rebuffed in a similar manner. "Trouble me not, I cannot arise and give thee." Now it was reaching out once more, this time to the A.I.M. "Because of his importunity, we will rise and give him as many as he needeth." (See Luke 11:5-9.)

As we got off the plane, a wave of humid heat engulfed us. We were glad that our fellow missionaries were at the airport to meet us. We had no problem getting through customs and immigration.

We were now in an entirely different world from the one we had left in Bunia. But the other missionaries had already prepared the way for us. They assured us that the Comorans were friendly. After all, where had these people ever seen doctors like Dick Anderson and Bill Barnett, who were not only top-notch professionally, but also showed genuine love for the people they had come to help?

Yet the missionaries seemed frustrated. Edythe and I had the job of bringing encouragement to them and helping to build a bridge between ourselves and the top officials. Our arrival seemed to perk up their spirits, but we were scared.

Our first objective was to get to the president. To get right to the top person on the totem pole had been our policy in Zaire, and it usually worked. Dr. Anderson and I went to the *chef de protocole* to arrange a rendezvous with the president. "You want to see the president?" chided the protocol chief. "He is a very busy man." Frustration number one. We got to see the minister of health and his first secretary, a satisfactory meeting, but we still wanted to see the president.

Some days later we managed an audience with the vice-president, who was friendly and cooperative. *"Monsieur le Vice-President,"* we asked, "can you arrange a rendezvous for us with the president?"

"The president is a very busy man, you know," answered the V.P., tapping the top of his beautifully carved desk with a Parker ballpoint pen as he pondered the problem. "I shall do my best to arrange this. You will hear from me." Some days later a message came from the V.P. The meeting was arranged.

Drs. Jim Propst and Harold De Souza, both from Kenya, were in Moroni with us at the time. They were there in the interests of an eye surgery program and an engineering project for water supply. They went with me, and we were ushered past a cordon of heavily armed soldiers. Only a few days before there had been an attempt made to assassinate the president. The attempted coup had failed, however, and Ali Soilihi was still very much in control.

As we entered his office, the president arose from behind his massive desk to greet us. He was the epitome of a gracious head of state. Chairs had been arranged for us. The V.P. and prime minister were also present, as well as a number of other ministers.

The president was cordial, but we could sense a barrier of suspicion. Who were these Americans and British who had come to his islands? Their professional work and conduct had been above reproach. The Comoran people were enthusiastic about the medical work. But what were these foreigners really up to? They must have an ulterior motive. We could feel the tension.

As I proceeded to give a report of the work that had been begun, and an outline of our plans and goals, the president was restless. His cultural background demanded that he show respect, but his inbred suspicion came into view. He asked abruptly, "Monsieur Brashler, who are you, and why have you come to these islands?"

The beads of nervous perspiration that stood out on my lips and forehead began to flow freely. My collar was soaked. I was at a disadvantage.

I immediately thought of the nearly 350,000 Comorans who had no knowledge of Christ. I also realized the import of the answer for which the president was waiting. Should I say the wrong thing, we could be ordered out of the country. Was I going to blow this opportunity? "Please help, Lord," I pleaded.

As I prayed silently, the words of our Lord flashed to mind. "And when you are brought unto the powers, take no thought

208

how or what ye shall answer. The Holy Spirit shall teach you what to say." Two other words also came to mind: "forthrightness," "frankness." The Lord wanted me to be honest. My wily nature was searching out diplomacy. The president's eyes were piercing as he waited for my answer.

"*Monsieur le président,*" I replied, "allow me to be frank and honest with you. You ask who we are. We are Christian missionaries. Our mission has worked in Africa for eighty-one years. We presently have more than 700 missionaries in six African countries. We have always maintained the best of relations with our host governments. We are also people who love the Lord Jesus Christ, whom you know as *Issu,* Allah's penultimate prophet. We believe him to be the Redeemer and Savior of sinners. He gives us peace and we have no fear of death. That is who we are.

"You also ask why we are here. It is our purpose to come to this beautiful country of yours to serve your people as an expression of our love for God. You need our professional help, and we are ready to give it with no ulterior motive. Although we are Christians, we have no intention of trying to christianize, or to westernize, your people. However, I say unabashedly that we do love Jesus Christ, and we are ready to talk about him on a person-to-person level with any who will listen."

Forthrightness and frankness. That was what the Lord had directed, and there it was. Now if we were kicked out it would be his responsibility.

The president sat very still, his dark eyes flashing. Did he like what I had told him? Was this to be the end of our Comoran outreach? As I waited for the president's response, I didn't know. It finally came.

"Monsieur Brashler, *vous êtes franc* (you are frank)."

"*Oui, Monsieur le président,* but isn't that what you want?"

"That is exactly what I want. I knew you were Christians, but I wanted to hear how you would answer my question. I appreciate your honesty. Now let me be the same with you. Your missionaries are our guests in a country that is 100 percent Muslim. There are no Comoran Christians here. I myself was born a Muslim, and I expect to die one. I pray as do all Mohammedans—five times daily with my face toward Mecca. I shall never become a Christian.

"But while I am a Muslim," continued the president, "I am also an educated and progressive man. I believe in the fundamental rights of the individual, one of which is the freedom of religion. If you Christians have anything to offer that will make better citizens out of us, then we are ready to listen to you.

"If a Comoran wants to abandon his faith in our prophet, he will be at liberty to do so. There will be no opposition from this government. Thank you for being honest with me. I want you all to feel welcome as our guests. I personally thank you for coming."

What was that again? Had I heard right? Yes, indeed I had. The president was smiling. His manner was relaxed. The smog of suspicion had cleared.

This enjoyable visit lasted almost an hour. It was a diplomatic success, and surely it was God's doing.

One week later we were again invited to see the president. This time Dr. and Mrs. Barnett came along. His Excellency was most happy to see the Barnetts, of whom he had heard so much. Another pleasant visit followed—and then came another bombshell. Rather brusquely he turned to me.

"Monsieur Brashler," he said, "with regard to our conversation last time, I have been thinking much of the question of religious freedom. I meant what I said, but I see a discrepancy. Our Muslim leaders use government facilities of Radio Comore to propagate their faith. In the interest of religious freedom, I want to give you the same privilege. You may have half an hour of free time each week for a Christian broadcast."

We thanked him profusely, and went home with a new job. Now, although totally inexperienced at that sort of thing, I was to become a radio broadcaster.

The program we put together could not be just any sort of Christian program but would have to be adapted to a Muslim country. The president was broad-minded, as were many of the educated people in the country, but the majority were fanatical Muslims. They hated Christianity and the Bible, and they would react violently to a message of redeeming love through *Issu*. We would have to employ a great deal of tact, drawing heavily upon the Old Testament and couching the message in unoffensive terms. A delicate assignment. We did not want to blow it, nor did we want to compromise our witness.

Within several weeks we had our first broadcast. The format was similar to that of a half-hour Christian program in America. We played music, the lively kind that the Comorans like; read passages of Scripture; and presented a gospel message—all in French. These programs were recorded on Saturday morning and broadcast without any editing on Sunday evening from 6:30 to 7:00. This time, suggested by the president, proved to be prime time.

Immediately there was listener response. Strangers stopped us on the street. "Are you the *pasteur* of *'Les Bonnes Nouvelles d'une Grande Joie'* (Good News of Great Joy, the title of the program)? You will continue it every Sunday, will you not? We listen with great interest."

Responses were gratifying. Children begged their parents to turn on the broadcast. Interest grew with each succeeding program, and we received only favorable reactions. There was violent opposition, too, but we remained ignorant of it. The opposition letters and calls all went to the president.

After four such broadcasts there came a registered letter from the director of Radio Comore. "By request of the president, the *'Bonnes Nouvelles'* program must adopt an entirely new format. From now on there is to be no more preaching, no more Bible passages, and no more music."

Satan was at work. Too much opposition had come to the president. After all, the bulk of his popular support came from Muslims. Somehow he would have to placate them. But without the Bible or music or a message, what was left?

I took the letter and went directly to the radio director. What did this letter mean? Was the program to be curtailed? After all, it was the president's idea that we have a Christian broadcast.

"*Mais non, monsieur,*" the director replied. "The program must continue. But from now on it will take the form of a dialogue. You will be assigned an interrogator who will ask certain questions, and you will answer from a biblical point of view. That will be more interesting to the public."

A dialogue might be less objectionable and embarrassing for the president, but for us it would be a setback. The popular appeal would be gone, and the well-prepared message would be missing. What to do?

"Mais oui, monsieur le directeur. If that is the president's wish, then we will do it his way," I replied halfheartedly. "We are his guests."

Saturday morning I was in the studio, seated at the microphone with one of the directors. He was to interrogate me. His first question after his opening statement was "Monsieur Brashler, what do you Christians believe to be the truth?"

My answer included reference to Pontius Pilate, who asked Jesus Christ a similar question, and also Jesus' words in John 14:6: "I am the way, the truth, and the life: no man cometh unto the Father, but by me."

"Then who is Jesus Christ?" pressed the director. Before I could answer the question he amplified it: "Is he God's Son?"

I knew I was in trouble. If anything angers a Muslim, it is to talk about God the Father and Jesus Christ his Son. My interrogator was out to embarrass me.

Again I appealed to heaven for divine wisdom in answering that crucial question. Again the Holy Spirit had his control system working. Again there beeped a familiar message: "Frankness and forthrightness." I was not to be evasive.

"Yes, Mr. Director, we Christians believe that Jesus Christ is God's Son."

"Eh bien," expostulated the director, "if Jesus is God's Son, then that means that God had a wife with whom he had sexual union. As a result, Jesus Christ was born. To us Muslims, that is an insult to Allah, who is righteous and holy and above such an act. We cannot accept that."

"I'm glad you do not believe that about Allah," I replied, "because that is not the way it was. We Christians don't believe that Allah had a wife. May I illustrate our belief by an example out of your own life? You are a Radio Comore director. As such, you play a very significant role in the life of your nation. You have heavy responsibilities in conditioning the thinking of your people and in educating them.

"But you are not confined to one role," I continued. "You are also the husband of your wife. You leave your office and step into an entirely different role, that of a husband. Again, you are a father, and there you step into a third role. You are one citizen, but you play three distinct roles.

"Now, do you think that God is inferior to man? True, he is the Creator/Judge wherein he exercises his omnipotence, holiness, and righteousness. We Christians believe precisely what you Muslims do regarding this role. But Allah is more than just that. He sees us as disobedient and banished sinners, and he wants to redeem us and bring us back into a place of fellowship with himself. In order to redeem us, Allah the Creator/Judge steps into the role of Allah the Redeemer. In order to be our Redeemer he must become a man—our kinsman Redeemer. By a creative act that he performed in the Virgin's womb, God became man when Jesus Christ was conceived and born. This was God stepping into his second role."

The interrogator sat in rapt attention. He asked many relevant and intelligent questions. It gave opportunity to bring out many truths that I hadn't dared to touch in previous broadcasts. God, in his sovereign way, was opening up opportunities to get the truth across.

The first dialogue was over. Despite the splendid opportunity to make clear some key truths that had been obscured to the Muslims for centuries, I was discouraged. The appeal of our broadcast was gone. Would young people continue to listen to such theological dialogue?

How wrong can one be? The next morning a visitor was at my office. We knew this young man well. He had worked for Frances Mumford, our British missionary, who had spent hours discussing these truths with him. He had also worked for Edythe, and she too had explained the Way to him. Now he wanted to see me.

"Monsieur," he started hesitantly, "I listened to your dialogue last evening, and I was tremendously interested in what you said concerning God's role as a Redeemer. Will you explain it to me again?"

Like Aquila and Priscilla with Apollos, we "expounded unto him the way of God more perfectly." That morning he accepted the Son of Allah as his Redeemer. At that time he was the only Comoran Christian in all of the islands. Since then he has identified himself with a band of Malagasy Christians in Moroni. He reads his Bible avidly. He prays.

For him it has cost to be a Christian. He has written us a number of times since our return to the United States. He wrote: "Thank you so much because you have not hidden the Truth from me. You have opened my eyes. Now I am born anew, and I am Christ's child. Be sure, *Monsieur et Madame*, that I shall never leave my Savior. He has saved me. He has died for my sins.

"It is very difficult for me to tell my parents and my friends that I am a Christian. When I tell my father that Christ is my Savior, he may kill me. He is a very strict Muslim. But I cannot continue to be a secret believer. I must share this good news, regardless of what happens. If I must die for my faith, I shall die happy."

Since writing that, this student has declared himself openly as a Christian. His father has beaten him severely and has turned him out of his home. Six other students have likewise confessed Christ as well as seven other adults. The six students were arrested and thrown into a cistern to wallow in the mud for several days without food. Through the intervention of the missionaries, the prisoners were released, but they are under constant surveillance.

Just before we left the islands, we were again invited to see the president. In our farewell meeting he said, "Convey to the Africa Inland Mission, and particularly to the missionaries who have come to the Comoros, my sincere thanks for their loving services. I have never seen professional help rendered with such genuine concern and love. I should really pay the salaries of all who have come to serve us, but you understand that our present economy will not permit that.

"However, before you leave, I want to show you my gratitude by placing my personal plane and pilot at your disposal. You will be given a tour of all the islands as my guests."

We regretted that our schedule did not allow us to accept his gracious offer. We had hoped that we might be able to return to the Comoros sometime later to accept the invitation. That seems very unlikely now. Ali-Soilihi was killed in the spring of 1978 by French mercenaries who now rule the islands. It had been the president's idea that dialogue should be held between educated men, where the tenets of the Koran would be objectively compared with those of the Bible. He thought that detente could be reached, and that we should be able to work together harmoniously.

More and more people, however, were becoming Christians among the Comorans. Fanatical Muslims were reacting violently. Two missionaries were arrested. In January 1978, just two years after the first missionaries entered the islands, all twenty of the team members felt constrained to leave the three independent islands. The fourth island, Mayotte, still under French control, allowed four single women to remain, at least for the time being, under the leadership of Dick and Dee Lasse, formerly missionaries to Zaire.

Africa Inland Mission's thrust into the exotic islands was short-lived, yet we have accepted the expulsion of the missionaries as an act of God's sovereign and perfect program. There are now twenty believers as a nucleus for the Comoran church. We commit them to God, knowing that his organism will grow and develop under the Holy Spirit's power. In our own case, the Comoro experience was some of the "very best wine," saved for the last of our overseas career.

Our thirty-six years in Africa took us over many thorny paths. It was a long road, with rough spots and pitfalls. Yet it was also a glory road, with many "rest stops" of joy and satisfaction. If we had it to do over again, we would gladly follow the same course. "Hitherto hath the Lord helped us."